To,

Anirudh

From,

Arpitha

This book belongs to

....

....

....

GLORIOUS
HISTORY OF
INDIA
FOR CHILDREN

ANURAG MEHTA

Nita Mehta
Enriching Young Minds

GLORIOUS
HISTORY OF
INDIA
FOR CHILDREN

© Copyright

Revised Hardbound Edition 2010

ISBN 978-81-7676-033-1

Illustrations:

Artist: Rajesh Parajapati

Layout and Laser Typesetting:

National Information
Technology Academy
3A/3, Asaf Ali Road
New Delhi-110002
☎ 23252948

Published by:

3A/3 Asaf Ali Road, New Delhi-110002
Tel: 91-11-23250091, 29214011, 23252948, 29218727
Fax: 91-11-29225218, 91-11-23250091
E-Mail : nitamehta@email.com
nitamehta@nitamehta.com
Website : http://www.nitamehta.com
http://www.snabindia.com

Contributing Writers:
Subhash Mehta
Tanya Mehta

Editorial & Proofreading:
Ekta
Deepali

Printed at:
MEHTA OFFSET

Distributed by:
NITA MEHTA BOOKS
3A/3, Asaf Ali Road,
New Delhi - 110 002
Tel.: 91-11-23252948, 23250091
Email: nitamehta@nitamehta.com

Price: Rs. 395/-

CONTENTS

Introduction...5

The Discovery of the Great Past...................6

The Aryans................................13

The Story of Rama.............................18

The Mahabharata............................ 26

Mahavira - the Conqueror of Soul............. 35

The Buddha.................................38

Alexander - the Great...........................45

Chandragupta Maurya............................ 48

Ashoka....................................... 52

The Mauryan Empire Breaks Up................58

The Kingdoms of South India....................62

The Gupta Kings..............................64

The Huns...................................68

The rule of Harshavardhan.........................69

Kings of the South..............................73

The Rise of Hinduism........................ 76

The Brave Rajputs............................78

The Invaders...............................82

The Invader becomes the King.................. 86

The Delhi Sultanate..................................88

Life of the People............................ 94

The New Religious Groups..................... 96

Babar - the Warrior............................ 99

Humayun - the Dreamer......................... 102

Akbar - the Great............................. 105

Jahangir - the Nature Lover.................. 110

Shah Jahan - the Builder...................... 113

Aurangzeb - the Cruel......................... 116

Shivaji - the Brave Maratha.................. 119

The Fall of the Mughal Empire.............. 126

The Marathas Become Stronger............. 127

The British in India......................... 129

Tipu Sultan.................................. 134

The Sikhs.................................... 137

The Revolt Against British Rule............ 145

Awakening of India........................... 152

Freedom Fighters.............................. 160

Mahatma Gandhi................................ 161

The Problems of Independent India........ 175

India, the Largest Democracy............... 176

Concluding Note From the Author.......... 179

INTRODUCTION

This book is an attempt to narrate the rich mythology and the glorious history of India. The historical events have been woven together to make an exciting book for children. These events are explained in simple language and are complemented with beautiful illustrations to capture the imagination of young readers.

The episodes have been carefully selected which will help to develop the personality of the child and give a bird's eye view of Indian history. The lessons from Indian history have been highlighted to impart wisdom to children to help them face day to day challenges of life. We have tried to cover events from thousands of years ago to the present day.

The great Indian epics of the Ramayana and the Mahabharata, the teachings of Buddha and Guru Nanak, the battles of the Mughals and the Marathas, the British rule and the great Indian struggle for independence have all been included in this book. History uses A.D. and B.C. to determine dates of events. B.C. stands for Before Christ and A.D. stands for Anno Domini which in Latin means in the year of our Lord (Christ). Historical dates are counted from the year of the birth of Christ.

Every child should read this book to understand our rich heritage and develop a sense of pride for our country.

THE DISCOVERY OF THE GREAT PAST

(Over 5,000 years ago)

Relics buried under the earth reveal the past

Some of the historical events that you will read in the book are more than 5,000 years old. Then how do we know about them? Many tools, weapons, pieces of pottery, beads, necklaces, pans and pots were found buried deep under the earth. These various discoveries tell us about the lives of people who used them and lived on this earth more than 5,000 years ago.

The discovery of Harappa and Mohenjo-Daro...

About a hundred and fifty years ago, some workers were building a railway line between Karachi and Lahore. While building the track, they found some bricks. The bricks were very good and the workers used them to build the tracks. They also realized that the bricks were very old. What they did not know was that these bricks were about 3,000 years old!

Later some people dug the earth in the place near the railway tracks. What they discovered with this digging caused great excitement, not only in India but also all over the world. They discovered that more than 5,000 years ago two very modern cities existed. These were the cities of **Harappa** and **Mohenjo-Daro**.

The Modern Cities of the bygone era...

Before the discovery of these cities - Harappa and Mohenjo-Daro, it was believed that India did not have a past of any great significance. It was believed that only in places like Egypt and Mesopotamia that great civilizations had flourished. In India, civilization was supposed to have existed only for the past 3,000 years. With the discovery of the Indus Valley civilization, the glorious past of India was revealed. We have come to know about how people lived 5,000 years ago.

Workers building the railway line

The life of the people…

The life of the people in those times was comfortable. The men wore robes which left one shoulder bare. The women wore beads and kept long hair. The children had a number of toys. Boys played with whistles, cart and wheeled toys while the girls played with dolls.

The people were engaged in different occupations such as farming, cattle rearing, pottery or carpentry. The seals found there tell us about the animals they reared and the Gods and Goddesses they worshipped. There were no weapons found in these cities. These people lived in peace and did not wish to conquer other lands.

The planned cities of the past

The Houses in the Cities...

The cities were built according to a plan. Houses were built of burnt bricks and were either single or double storeyed. There were small houses having one or two rooms and big houses having several rooms. All houses had a courtyard, bathroom and drains to carry the dirty water away. Houses were built on both sides of the street. The streets were broad and straight so that bullock carts and people could move easily.

Did You Know?
Before the discovery of Harappa & Mohenjo-daro, it was believed that only in places like Egypt and Mesopotamia that great civilizations had flourished.

The Great Bath House

The Great Bath House

The most important building that has been found in the city of Mohenjo-Daro is a Great Bath House. This was like a large swimming pool measuring 55 meters long and 33 meters wide. It had a few steps which led to the floor of the pool. There was a well to supply fresh water and drainage to empty the tank. Broad corridors on four sides with a number of rooms surrounded the pool.

The Forgotten Lands...

Earlier it was thought that Mohenjo-Daro, Harappa and some other cities discovered later, were built only along the river Indus. But new research has shown that nearly two-thirds of the sites were along another river, Saraswati, which is now extinct. Accordingly archeologists have renamed the civilization as **Indus-Saraswati Civilization**. The land through which the river Indus flows was once a part of India but some years ago this land was separated from India and became part of a new country called Pakistan.

What really happened to the great Indus Valley people, no one really knows. Some believe that violent tribes coming from elsewhere conquered them. Others think that the Great Indian Dessert crept slowly in forcing the people to move elsewhere. Years went by and their cities lay buried under the sand. Now, slowly their story is being dug out from beneath the ground revealing a lot of surprises!

 LESSONS TO LEARN...

Indians are Very Intelligent

Even 5,000 years ago, Indian people lived in planned cities, made houses of bricks and used woven clothes and toys. Around the same time, most people in other parts of the world were like wild animals who lived in caves, wore animal skins, used stones as weapons and ate raw meat. This proves that the Indian people were peace loving, far more intelligent and advanced than most people living in other parts of the world.

*People living in India
more that 5,000 years ago*

*People living in other parts of the world
more than 5,000 years ago*

THE ARYANS
(The Warrior Tribe)

The Aryans

The Northern boundary of India is formed by the Himalayas, the highest mountains in the world. Although it seems impossible to enter India from the north because of this formidable barrier, yet from time to time, visitors have made their way to our country from the north. These people made use of little gaps in the mountains called passes, to cross them.

The Aryans were among the first people to arrive in India. They are believed to have come from the plains of Central Asia perhaps in search of better pastures for their flocks and more fertile land to grow.

When the Aryans arrived, there were already other people living in India. Their way of life was different from that of the Aryans. The Aryans rode horses and used swords as weapons. They pushed the original inhabitants out of their land. But as time went by, the Aryans and the other people became friends and began to live together in peace.

The life of the Aryans...

We have a lot of information about the Aryans from the books called the **Vedas**. These books are the oldest books in the world and were written in Sanskrit. By studying the *Vedas* carefully, we have come to know a lot about the Aryan people's lives and customs.

The Aryans were divided into three groups –

1. The warriors
2. The priests
3. The cultivators

The people were divided into these groups on the basis of their occupation and not by birth.

The Priests Performing Yagnas

The beginning of Hinduism...

During this period, a new religion **Hinduism** started in India. The followers of Hinduism were called **Hindus**. The Hindus believed in the worship of many Gods. The most popular Hindu Gods were Brahma (the creator), Vishnu (the preserver) and Shiva (the destroyer). The Hindus also believed in performing *Yagnas* and offering sacrifices to the Gods. Elaborate rituals were performed at the birth of a child, at marriage and at death. Cows, horses, gold and cloth were given to the priests as gifts. The priests were considered the link between man and God. Their power and influence over society increased.

Division of Society...

As time passed the priest and the warriors began to consider themselves superior to the cultivators and other people. Their false superiority made them believe that there were some people whom they should totally avoid. These people came to be known as the **Untouchables**. This resulted in a new division of society.

Brahmins (Highest Caste)

The new classes or categories are listed below in order of their importance in society with the priest (Brahmin) being the most powerful and the Untouchable being the weakest. The classes are as follows:

1. **The Brahmins (priests)**

2. **The Kshatriyas (warriors)**

3. **The Vaishyas (business people)**

4. **The Shudras (labourers, workers etc.,)**

5. **The Untouchable (lowest caste)**

Kshatriyas

The division of people into these classes was on the basis of birth and not by occupation. This division was known as the caste system. This was hereditary and the upper caste exploited the lower caste. The **caste system** was so rigid that people belonging to different castes could not marry each other.

Vaishyas

Shudras

This division of society was very shameful and sad as this promoted the belief that some human beings are better than the others.

In the course of time, the Aryans established powerful kingdoms throughout the north of India. The south of India had its own people. They were called the **Dravidians**. They had their own kingdoms and cities and people who spoke a different language and followed different customs.

For a long time, the Aryans and the Dravidians remained quite apart from each other. But as time passed, the Aryans, especially their sages, began to visit the south. There was an exchange of customs and languages and in due course of time the people of the north and the south mingled with each other and began to live in the same way.

Untouchables

THE STORY OF RAMA

(The oldest Indian epic)

The oldest and the most popular Indian epic is perhaps that related to Rama and Sita. This wonderful epic is called the **Ramayana** and was written by a sage (saadhu) called **Valmiki**. Some scholars believe that the story of Rama's adventures, is a story of the Aryans slowly moving into South India.

RAMAYAN

Many, many years ago, Ayodhya was a beautiful city ruled by a powerful king, Dashratha, who had three queens and four sons. Rama was the son of the eldest queen Kaushalya. Kaikeyi's son was Bharata and the sons of Sumitra were Lakshmana and Shatrughana.

As Ram was the eldest and the ablest of the four sons, Dashratha wanted him to be the king after him. But Rama's step-mother, Kaikeyi, wanted her own son, Bharata, to become the king. She tricked the old king into sending Rama to the forest for fourteen years. Rama, being the obedient son, did not hesitate at once to follow his father's command and left for the Dandaka forest at the foot of the Vindhya mountains. He was accompanied by his wife, Sita and brother, Lakshmana.

Dashratha with Kaikeyi

Rama, Sita & Lakshmana in forest

Back in Ayodhya everybody was sad. King Dashratha was so upset that he died of grief. Bharata who loved his brother Rama very much, refused to sit on the throne. He placed Rama's slippers on the seat of the throne. He himself sat at the foot of the throne and managed the affairs of the state in Rama's name.

Lakshmana cuts off
Surpanakha's nose

In the forest, life for Rama, Sita and Lakshmana was very hard. They had none of the comforts they enjoyed at the palace and faced hardship and danger at every step. Rama and Lakshmana had to fight many *rakshasas* or demons who tried to harm them.

One day, Surpanaka, the sister of the demon-king Ravana, saw Lakshmana. She liked him and wanted to marry him. Lakshmana did not want to marry her. But Surpanaka wouldn't let him go. Lakshmana was so angry that he cut her nose off with his sword.

Surpanaka ran to her brother Ravana and told him what Lakshmana had done to her. On hearing this, Ravana became very furious. He made a wicked plan and called Mareecha, his uncle and sent him to Rama's hut disguised as a beautiful golden deer.

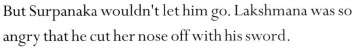

Sita is charmed by the Golden Deer

Ravana carrying off Sita

When Sita saw the golden deer she was so charmed by it that she wanted it for her own. She pleaded to Rama to get it for her. Reluctantly, Rama went after the deer and Lakshmana stayed back at the hut to guard Sita. After a while they heard Rama's shout to Lakshmana for help.

On hearing this, Sita became anxious. She asked Lakshmana to go for Rama's help. Lakshmana did not want to leave Sita alone in the forest. But on Sita's insistence he had to go out to help Rama. But Rama had not called out for help at all. It was the cunning Mareecha who had imitated Rama's voice. Both Sita and Lakshmana had been tricked.

All along Ravana had been hiding in the bushes. As soon as Lakshmana left, he caught hold of Sita and carried her off to his kingdom. An old bird named Jatayu tried to stop Ravana but was ruthlessly killed in the pursuit.

Rama could not capture the deer as there was no deer at all!

When Rama and Lakshmana returned to the hut empty-handed, they found Sita gone. Rama knew at once that a cruel trick had been played upon him. He was stricken with grief but vowed to search for Sita and bring her back.

The Monkeys help Rama...

After many days of search, the two brothers met Sugriva, the king of the monkeys. Sugriva and his minister Hanuman promised to help them find Sita.

The bridge to Lanka

Did You Know?
Even today the incomplete staircase to heaven can be seen in the island of Lanka known today as Sri Lanka.

23

Rama kills Ravana

It was soon discovered that Sita was being held prisoner by Ravana on the Island of Lanka. The army of monkeys brought large stones and built a bridge across the sea for Rama to cross over to the Island. Once on the island, Rama fought the ten-headed demon king Ravana and killed him. Rama and Sita were together again. The fourteen years of Rama's stay in the forest too had come to an end. He returned to Ayodhya with his wife and brother. Rama was crowned the king of Ayodhya and ruled for many years.

LESSONS TO LEARN...

All that glitters is not Gold

Sita was attracted towards the unreal golden deer which was a demon in disguise. She got fooled by the outer appearance and did not even listen to Rama. Ravana took advantage of this and abducted Sita. Thus, it is truly said, "All that glitters is not gold."

Good Always Wins over Evil

Ravana was a great and powerful king and had a huge army but still lost to Rama and the army of monkeys. This proves that good always wins over evil.

Ravana was a great king but his one evil deed resulted in his fall. It is said that Ravana performed many good deeds, offered many sacrifices to the Gods and the Gods were also very pleased with him. Ravana wanted to live in heaven and was building a staircase to heaven. It is believed that his every good deed resulted in one additional stair in the staircase. But his one evil deed resulted in his fall and closed his entry into heaven.

Even today the incomplete staircase to heaven can be seen in the island of Lanka which is known today as Sri Lanka.

THE MAHABHARATA

(The Great Indian War- more than 3,000 years ago)

The Mahabharata is another world famous epic. It is about the Pandavas and their cousins, the Kauravas, and the great war they fought for the throne of Hastinapur. Vyasa was the sage (saadhu) who wrote the Mahabharata. The story of the Mahabharata is told in the form of a great poem. It contains one lac verses and is the longest poem in the world.

MAHABHARATA

One of the most famous kingdoms of ancient India was that of the Kurus. They had their capital at Hastinapur on the banks of the river Ganga. When Pandu, the king of Hastinapur, died, his eldest son was very young. So his brother Dhritarashtra, a blind old man, became the king.

The Kauravas

Dhritarashtra had a hundred sons and they were known as the Kauravas. The eldest Kaurava was Duryodhana and the second eldest was Dushasana.

Pandu had five sons and they were known as the Pandavas. Their mother was Kunti. The eldest of the Pandava was Yudhishthira. The second was Bheem who was known for his amazing strength. He ate great quantities of food and could uproot trees with his bare hands! Arjuna, the third brother, was a skillful archer and a brave warrior. The twins, Nakula and Sahdeva were the youngest. Though the princes grew up together, the Kauravas were jealous of the Pandavas. Duryodhana wanted to be the next king but he knew that Yudhishthira was the rightful heir and would eventually become the king. Duryodhana told his father Dhritarashtra to make him the king but the blind king said, "No son, that cannot be. I too want you to become the king but Yudhishthira is the heir to the throne. The people also love him because he is kind, brave and truthful. I cannot go against the wishes of the people." On hearing this, Duryodhana became angry and thought of a plan to kill the Pandavas.

The Pandavas

27

The Pandavas along with their mother Kunti were sent to Varnavarta, a beautiful city on the banks of a river. They were given a beautiful palace to live in but the palace was made of wax and other things that burn easily. Duryodhana's plan was to set fire to the palace and kill the Pandavas by burning them alive.

But the Pandavas got to know about Duryodhana's evil plan and managed to escape from the palace. The Pandavas did not go to Hastinapur but instead went away to seek their own fortune. For the next one year they traveled by night and rested by day to escape the notice of people.

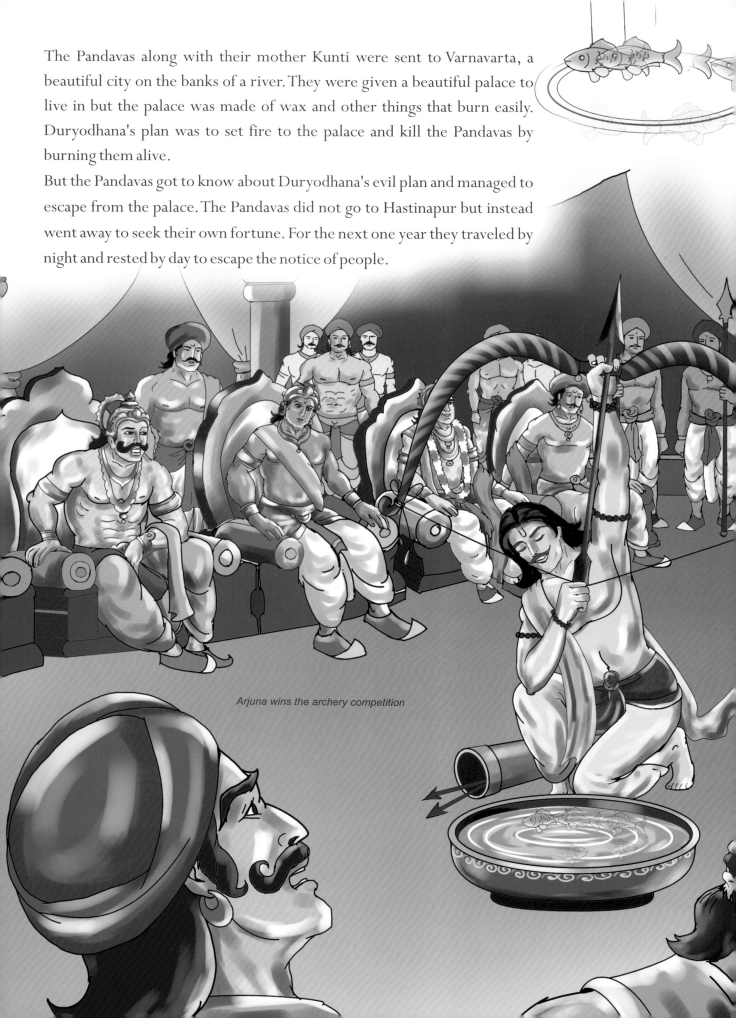

Arjuna wins the archery competition

The neighbours of the Kauravas were the Panchalas. They were known for their courage and learning. The Panchala king, Drupada, had a beautiful daughter called Draupadi. She was to choose herself a husband from among the most skillful warriors of the time. For this, the king had arranged an archery contest. When this news reached the Pandavas, Bheema and Yudhishthira told Arjuna to participate in the contest.

The Pandavas reached King Drupada's palace on the day of the contest. The palace was full of princes and kings who had come to participate in the contest.

Did You Know?
Mahabharata is the world's longest poem having one lac verses.

When everyone was seated, the King said, "I have set a test. The man who wins the test, marries my daughter. Near the big bowl of water, there is a bow. Directly overhead on the ceiling is a golden fish revolving at high speed. The man who wants to marry my daughter, must first string the bow and then hit the eye of the fish with one arrow. This he must do by looking at its reflection in the water."

The princes and the kings present in the palace tried their luck but no one could win the contest. When everyone failed, Arjuna got up and walked towards the bow. He knelt down in front of the bowl of water, took careful aim and shot an arrow at the fish. It hit the eye of the fish.

Arjuna won the contest and married Draupadi. With great delight, the Pandavas returned home with Draupadi. When they reached home their mother Kunti was inside one of the rooms.

"Mother," they called, "come and see what we have brought with us."

"I'm busy now. Share whatever you have brought," Kunti answered not knowing what it was.

Game of Dice

On hearing this, the brothers were confused. They had never disobeyed their mother and neither could they do it then. So, Draupadi became the wife of all the five brothers.

The Pandavas now decided to return to Hastinapur. Within a few days, the Pandavas arrived at Hastinapur with their mother. Dhritarashtra felt sorry that the Pandavas had to wander homeless for so long. He divided the kingdom into two parts and gave one part to his sons and the other to the Pandavas. Although it was a raw deal for the Pandavas as they got the rocky and desert part of the kingdom but they still did not lose hope. They worked day and night and converted the desert land into a beautiful city. The city was named Indraprastha as it was as beautiful as Lord Indra's city in heaven. The fame of this city spread far and wide and people flooded to it. Many settled there and Yudhishthira's kingdom grew rich and prosperous.

The fame of Indraprastha and the Pandavas made Duryodhana very jealous. Duryodhana made a wicked plan to snatch their kingdom from them. Duryodhana challenged Yudhishthira to a game of dice. In those days, a king could not refuse such a challenge. Yudhishthira played and lost everything he had - his palace, his horses, his wealth and eventually his entire kingdom. He staked himself and his brothers and lost them too. Then he staked Draupadi and lost yet again. Dushasana, Duryodhana's younger brother, dragged Draupadi by her hair into the court. The Pandavas hung their heads in shame as the Kauravas rejoiced. Helpless, Draupadi prayed to Lord Krishna and was saved from disgrace.

Dhritarashtra could not bear to see what had happened and gave back the Pandavas their kingdom. But the wicked Duryodhana could not digest this. He challenged Duryodhana to another game of dice. This time the condition was that the losers had to spend twelve years in the forest and one more year in hiding without being found out. Yudhishthira lost yet again and the Pandavas with Draupadi went away to the forest.

The Pandavas spent the thirteen years in extreme hardship. When they returned, Duryodhana refused to give back their kingdom. He told them that if they want their kingdom back they have to fight for it. The Pandavas had no choice but to fight.

Did You Know?
It is believed that the battle of Kurukshetra was fought around 1190 B.C.

Krishna giving message to Arjuna

Preparations of the war between the Kauravas and the Pandavas began. The two armies assembled on the battlefield of Kurukshetra. On the morning of the battle, the armies stood facing each other. Krishna was Arjuna's charioteer. When Arjuna saw Dronacharya (the Guru of Pandavas and Kauravas), his cousins, granduncles and uncles on the other side, he became upset. He said, "Krishna, what is the use of this war? We are going to fight our own people. We may kill them. Isn't that a sin?"

Krishna smiled and said, "Your cousins have done wrong to you. They are unjust. They have taken away your kingdom and you must fight to take it back."

"But I don't want the kingdom by killing my own people," argued Arjuna. Krishna said, "Arjuna, always remember that it is not whom you fight that is important but what you fight for. Even if your own people are on the other side, you must still fight for truth and justice. This is not just a war between the Kauravas and the Pandavas, this is a war between good and evil."

Krishna explained many things about life, death, truth, justice and so on. He managed to clear the confusion in Arjuna's mind and prepared him to fight the battle. All the teachings of Krishna are found in the sacred book of the Hindus, the **Bhagvad Gita**.

The End of War and the Victory of Good over Evil...

The war began. The armies of the Pandavas and the Kauravas consisted of thousands of men, horses and elephants. Both the armies fought fiercely and a large number of men were killed on both sides. After 18 days of fierce fighting, finally the great Kaurava army was defeated. Yudhishthira was crowned the king of Hastinapur and justice prevailed.

LESSONS TO LEARN...

Always fight for truth & justice

For justice, even if you have to fight with your near and dear ones, do not hesitate to do so. Always stand for your rights. Do your duty well without worrying about the results.

Gambling is a very evil practice

Gambling only leads to destruction. We have seen how the good Yudhishthira lost his mind under the evil influence of gambling. He not only lost his kingdom but also his self respect and dignity. He not only suffered himself but also made his wife and brothers suffer at the cruel hands of Duryodhana.

While gambling, either you are winning or losing, it is very difficult to stop and not play more. Thus, it is best to avoid gambling.

MAHAVIRA -THE CONQUEROR OF SOUL

(599 B.C. - 527 B.C. - more than 2,500 years ago)

A prince, named Vardhamana, was born in 599 B.C. Before his birth, his mother had many dreams. These dreams showed auspicious signs and announced the coming of a very special baby. Until about the age of thirty, Vardhamana led a life of comfort. He was married and had a daughter. But soon he left his home and family and went in search of knowledge. He gave up every possession he owned, even the clothes covering his body. For twelve years, he roamed from place to place and faced many hardships. Then, one day, after meditating for two and a half days, he had a deep religious experience. He found what he had been looking for. He then came to be known as **Mahavira**, or the great soul, and *Jina*, the Conqueror.

The Birth of a New Religion..

Mahavira travelled far and wide to share his ideas with others. He taught that everything in the universe, including trees, stones and even water has a soul. The aim of life should be to make one's soul pure. The soul can be made pure by following the path of righteousness - right faith, right knowledge and right conduct. By right conduct he meant not telling lies, not stealing, not injuring living beings and not being greedy.

Statue of Mahavira

35

The followers of Mahavira came to be known as **Jains** and the religion founded by him is known as **Jainism**. Since everything has a soul, much care had to be taken to avoid killing even an ant. Jain monks went about with a muslin cloth over their mouths to avoid tiny insects from entering their mouths by mistake and losing their lives. The teachings of Jainism became very popular among some people, particularly the traders and merchants. This was natural since the other groups like the *Kshatriyas* could hardly practice the vow of non-violence, just as the farmers could not avoid killing pests and insects while going about their work.

Mahavira spreads his message

Mahavira died at the age of seventy two in 527 B.C. By then he had 14,000 followers and many more Jains became after that. About two hundred years after Mahavira's death, a group of Jains left for the south as there was a great famine in north India. There they spread and followed Mahavira's teachings. These people came to be known as the *Digambaras*, as they went about naked. The *Digambara* sect of Jains believe that during and after enlightenment Mahavira wore no clothes. So the *Digambara* sadhus wear no clothes. They have renounced all worldly possessions.

The northern Jains form the *Svetambara* sect of Jainism. The *Svetambaras* believe that after gaining enlightenment Mahavira wore no worldly materials or clothes. However, it was Lord Indra who covered him with a white cloth afterwards. So, the *Svetambaras* wear a pristine white cloth like shawl.

Did You Know?
Mahavira's followers were mostly the traders and the merchants as the Kshatriyas could not practice the vow of non-violence and the farmers could not avoid killing pests and insects.

THE BUDDHA

(567 B.C. - 487 B.C.-more than 2,500 years ago)

Siddhartha was the son of King Shuddhodana and his wife Maya. When Siddhartha was only five years old, his mother died. As the boy grew up, his father tried his best to keep Siddhartha happy. The King had three different palaces for three different seasons built for his son. The little prince had everything he wanted. He wore the finest clothes, ate the best food and played with fascinating toys. But as he grew up, he became less and less fond of these things. Siddhartha liked being alone and spent most of his time in deep thinking. There were lots of thoughts in his mind and he felt troubled and uneasy.

Prince Siddhartha learns about suffering...

Later Prince Siddhartha was married to a beautiful princess called Yashodhara. Soon they had a son whom they named Rahul. Even this did not cheer up Siddhartha.

One day, Siddhartha was driving through the streets in his royal chariot. He first saw an old man and then a sick man whose back was so bent that he could hardly walk. On seeing this, Siddhartha was confused. He asked the charioteer (driver), "What is wrong with these people?" The charioteer answered, "These people are old and sick. They are suffering as this is the way of life."

The sights that changed Prince Siddhartha

Siddhartha could not understand why men should grow old or suffer. Then he saw a dead body being carried. He became very upset. Siddhartha had never seen such sights inside the palace. He was shocked to see so much unhappiness in the world. For the first time he came to know that all men must indeed suffer, grow old and die. As the charioteer turned back towards the palace, he saw an old monk. The monk was wearing yellow robes and had a begging bowl in his hand. This man appeared most at peace in the midst of the misery all around him.

Siddhartha was very confused and he decided that he would not rest until he found out why there was so much suffering in the world and how people could be free from it. One night, while his wife slept with their little son, Siddhartha left his home.

Siddhartha went into the forest to search for a way out of suffering and sorrow, not just for himself but for all mankind. For six years he denied himself all comfort and kept wandering from place to place. He starved himself for forty days but still did not find his answers. Siddhartha knew that as long as he stayed at home enjoying the comfort of the palace he would never be able to find answers to his questions.

Siddhartha becomes Buddha...

Siddhartha started meditating under a peepal tree in Bodh Gaya. He thought deeply about the things that disturbed him. For 49 days, he meditated and then, suddenly, one day he himself found all the answers. He felt as if he had learned all the secrets of the world.

Now that Siddhartha had knowledge, he began to spread his knowledge to other people. People were very influenced with Siddhartha's teachings. Soon Siddhartha came to be known as the **Buddha** which means *the one who has knowledge*.

Siddhartha becomes Buddha

Buddha taught that greed and selfishness is cause of all the sorrow and unhappiness in the world. If you want to be free of sorrow and unhappiness, you must be free from greed and desire. Buddha said that to be free from greed and desire people should follow the Eight-Fold Path. The Eight-Fold Path consisted of right views, right resolve, right speech, right conduct, right livelihood, right effort, right recollection and right meditation.

Buddha said that all men were equal and he did not believe in the caste system. No one belongs to the upper or lower caste by birth. It is only your deeds that determine your caste. Buddha travelled from place to place to spread his knowledge. Buddha spoke in simple words and in a language which the common people understood. He loved everyone and everyone was welcome to follow his teachings.

The Spread of Buddhism...

Many men and women followed Buddha's teachings in their day to day life and became monks and nuns.

Thus, the new religion Buddhism was born. Buddhist monks give up most possessions. They keep only their saffron yellow robes, a needle, a razor, a water strainer, and a begging bowl. Monks spend their time praying, teaching, and meditating.

Buddhists believe that everyone is reborn after death. The quality of their new life depends on their deeds (Karma). Karma is the total of all the good and bad deeds they did in the life they have just left. Buddha died at the age of eighty in 487 B.C. The Buddhist monks and nuns spread the new religion beyond India's borders into countries such as Sri Lanka, China, Japan, Burma, Bhutan and Tibet.

The spread of Buddhism

❧ LESSONS TO LEARN... ❧

Free yourself from greed and desire

All the suffering and unhappiness in the world is caused by excessive greed and desire. This desire of wanting more makes one selfish and dissatisfied. True happiness can only be achieved by selflessly helping the poor and the needy. Work hard, help others and concentrate on being satisfied and happy.

ALEXANDER - THE GREAT

(356 B.C. - 323 B.C.)

Alexander, the great

Alexander was the king of Macedon (Greece). He was very brave and ambitious. His dream was to conquer the whole world. At the age of 26 (in 330 B.C.), Alexander conquered the whole of Syria, Palestine, Egypt and Persia. At that time, India was made up of a number of small kingdoms. Crossing the Hindukush mountains, Alexander entered Punjab (India) in 326 B.C. During that period, there were two powerful kings in Punjab, namely, Ambhi and Porus.

Ambhi, the king of Taxila...

Ambhi, the king of Taxila was scared of Alexander and refused to fight him. Instead, he welcomed Alexander and offered him gifts. Alexander was very pleased with him.

The brave, self respecting Porus...

Alexander now ordered Porus to come and meet him. Porus was a brave and self respecting king. He replied, "Alexander, I will certainly meet you. But not in Taxila. I will meet you on the battlefield."

Alexander meets the king of Taxila

Alexander defeats Porus...

Porus's army met Alexander's army on the banks of the Jhelum river. The two armies were on opposite banks of the river. At night, when it was raining heavily, Alexander's army crossed the river and launched a sudden attack. Porus's army was taken by surprise and was slow in fighting back. By evening, it was all over and a wounded Porus was brought in chains before Alexander.

"How shall I treat you?" asked Alexander proudly.

"Like a king," replied the equally proud Porus.

Alexander was very impressed with his courage and self respect. Alexander ordered his soldiers to release Porus at once and gave his kingdom back to him.

LESSONS TO LEARN...

Courage and self respect can win over even enemies

A person who does not lose his courage and self respect even in the most difficult situation always wins in the end. Even though Porus lost the battle he was treated with respect by Alexander and his kingdom was returned to him.

The death of Alexander...

Now, Alexander set his sight on other kingdoms. He wanted to go further and conquer other kingdoms but his soldiers refused to do so as they were very tired. Alexander left behind some of his Greek generals to look after the territories he had conquered and with the rest of his army turned back towards Macedon. But he never reached Macedon. Alexander died on his way back in Babylon (modern Iraq) in 323 B.C. Alexander was only 33 years old at the time of his death.

Alexander and Porus

CHANDRAGUPTA MAURYA

(321 B.C. - 298 B.C.)

When Alexander left India, his Greek officers stayed behind to look after the territories he had conquered. But with Alexander's sudden death, his officers also left India. There was disorder and confusion in the northwest part of India.

During this period, there lived a young, adventurous man who had dreams of becoming a great conqueror like Alexander. His name was Chandragupta Maurya. He had been watching the situation carefully and thought that the situation was ideal to fulfill his dream.

Dhanananda insults Chandragupta

Dhanananda insults Chandragupta...

Magadh (Bihar) was a powerful kingdom ruled by Dhanananda. Chandragupta Maurya was a general (chief of soldiers) in Dhanananda's army.

One day, Dhanananda became angry with Chandragupta and insulted him. Chandragupta left his army and went to Punjab.

Chandragupta meets Chanakya...

After wandering homeless for some time, Chandragupta met a very clever Brahmin (priest) named Chanakya. Chanakya had been a minister in the court of Dhanananda. He too was insulted by Dhanananda and was determined to take revenge from him. The two became friends and made plans to conquer Magadh.

Chandragupta attacks kingdoms of the North-West...

Chandragupta first attacked the weak kingdoms of the northwest. These kingdoms were deserted by the Greek officers and were without a leader. Having conquered these kingdoms, Chandragupta decided to conquer Magadh. But Magadh was a vast and powerful kingdom. It was not easy to capture it.

Chandragupta meets Chanakya

Chandragupta learns a lesson

Chandragupta learns a lesson...

Once Chandragupta saw a mother scolding her child for eating from the centre of the plate. "The food is very hot in the centre," scolded the mother "Do not eat from there, you'll burn your mouth. Eat from the sides of the dish where the food is cooler."

This incident gave Chandragupta the idea to conquer Magadh. He first decided to attack the corners of the kingdom and then move slowly inside towards the capital (centre of the kingdom), Pataliputra. His plan worked and in 326 B.C., Chandragupta was crowned the king of Magadh.

During that period, one of Alexander's generals, Seleukos, had become master of most of the kingdoms that Alexander had conquered. With a large army, Seleukos, marched into Punjab with an aim to conquer it. He met Chandragupta's army in battle and was defeated by him. He was forced to give Chandragupta not only a large part of Afghanistan, but also his daughter in marriage.

Later, when there was peace between them, an ambassador from Seleukos's court visited Pataliputra.

His name was **Megasthenes** and he wrote a book called **Indika** in which he described all he saw during his stay. Chanakya also wrote a book titled **Arthashastra**. From these two books, we gather a lot about the times of Chandragupta Maurya.

Chanakya's intelligent ideas combined with Chandragupta's fighting skills brought them victory. Chandragupta became the ruler of a great empire and lived in a grand palace surrounded by a group of armed women. Chandragupta ruled his kingdom well and undertook many activities for the welfare of the people. He built many hospitals, dams and canals. Roads were built connecting important cities. Chandragupta ruled his kingdom for 24 years and then towards the end of his reign, he became a follower of Jainism. He handed over the throne to his son Bindusara and accompanied by Jain monks, left for south India. There he died a peaceful death.

Mauryan coins

Did You Know?
Chandragupta lived in a grand palace surrounded by a group of armed women.

LESSONS TO LEARN...

A powerful enemy can be defeated by using your intelligence and courage The brave Chandragupta and the clever Chanakya were able to conquer the powerful kingdom of Magadh using their courage and intelligence.

ASHOKA

(The Greatest King of India. 273 B.C. - 232 B.C.)

Bindusara (298 B.C. - 273 B.C.) was an able king and expanded the Mauryan empire. He ruled for twenty five years but not much is known about him. He was probably a great general and a good ruler because by the end of his reign, the Mauryan empire included the whole of India, except for the extreme southern part and Kalinga (Orissa) in the east.

Ashoka was the son of Bindusara and inherited this great empire around 272 B.C. Ashoka was very ambitious and decided to conquer Kalinga.

Battle of Kalinga (261 B.C.)...

Ashoka attacked Kalinga with a huge army. The people of Kalinga fought bravely. It was a terrible war in which more than one lac people were killed and more than two lac people were wounded. It was a crushing defeat for Kalinga and Ashoka became the king of almost the whole of India. This was the first time in Indian history that such a large area was under a single ruler.

Did You Know?
In the battle of Kalinga over one lac people were killed & over two lac were wounded.

Ashoka attacks Kalinga

However, this victory did not make Ashoka happy. He was very sad when he saw the destruction and suffering the war had caused. The sight of so many dead bodies and the cries of widows and orphans made him unhappy. He blamed himself for all the suffering and decided never to fight another war.

King Ashoka becomes a Buddhist...

Ashoka became a Buddhist and devoted his life to the welfare of his people. He gave up hunting and killing of animals and followed the path of nonviolence.

The battle of Kalinga was a turning point in Ashoka's life. Before this battle, Ashoka was considered a ruthless king and people called him *Chanda* (Devil) Ashoka. Later, when Ashoka followed the path of nonviolence and kindness, people started calling him *Dharma* (Virtuous) Ashoka.

The destruction of Kalinga

Ashoka becomes a Buddhist

Statue of Buddha

Ashoka Pillar at Sarnath

Ashoka spreads his message...

Ashoka wanted his people to be honest and kind. But since his kingdom was very large, he himself could not go and talk to all his people. So he got his messages carved on pillars of stones and put them up in every corner of the country. These writings or **edicts** as they are called were in Pali, the language of the common people of that time. These asked the people to be kind and honest. Ashoka visited all the places connected with Buddha's life. He put up a pillar to mark the place where Buddha was born. He built many *viharas* or places where Buddhist holy men could live. In fact, he built so many of these that Magadh came to be known as the country of viharas or Bihar, as it is called today. One of Ashoka's pillar at Sarnath, near Varnasi has the figure of four lions sitting back to back on the top. This forms the official seal of the Indian government today. Ashoka had ruled the country not by force but according to *dhamma* or the law of piety. A commonly seen symbol in Ashoka's edicts is a wheel. This wheel stands for *dhamma*.

Ashoka, the Great...

As a result of Ashoka's efforts, Buddhism became popular not only in India, but it also spread to many countries of South-East Asia. Buddhism became a world religion. Ashoka believed in nonviolence and equality of all religions. He never forced his people to follow Buddhism. He was very concerned about the welfare of the people and built many hospitals and rest houses for them.

The people in his kingdom were happy and prosperous. For these reasons, Ashoka is known as the greatest king of India. Ashoka died about the year 232 B.C. and his death resulted in the dis-integration of the Mauryan empire.

LESSONS TO LEARN...

WAR LEADS TO SORROW. PEACE LEADS TO JOY.

Ashoka conquered the whole of India but still did not find peace or happiness. It was only when he followed the path of nonviolence and kindness, he experienced peace and happiness and is now remembered as the greatest king of India.

Viharas

THE MAURYAN EMPIRE BREAKS UP

(Indian History From 200 B.C. - A.D. 300)

After Ashoka's death, the Mauryan Empire broke up into many smaller kingdoms. The rulers after Ashoka were not strong enough to hold together the large empire. Kalinga, which was conquered by Ashoka was the first to break away and the others followed. Then one day, the last Mauryan king Brihadratha was killed by his own general Pushyamitra Sunga.

The Kingdoms of the Indo-Greeks...

The whole of North-West India was ruled by foreigners. After the death of Alexander his generals settled in India. These Greek generals occupied the North-West of India. These rulers came to be known as Indo-Greeks. The most famous Indo-Greek king was Menander. He ruled his kingdom well and was famous for his sense of justice. He was always open to new ideas. After having a discussion with the Buddhist scholar Nagasena, he was so impressed that he became a follower of Buddha.

The Tribes of Central Asia…

Just as the Greeks had forced their way into India, the tribes from Central Asia also entered India. The Shakas arrived first followed by the Pahlavas towards the first century B.C.

Another tribe that came to India was the Kushanas. This was about the time that Jesus Christ was born. The Kushanas were the nomads from China. They defeated the Shakas and Pahlavas and settled in Kashmir and Afghanistan.

The greatest Kushana king was Kanishka. He fought many wars and conquered many kingdoms. His kingdom extended from Central Asia to the borders of Bengal. His capital was Peshawar.

The Indo-Greeks

59

Kanishka met with the great Buddhist scholar Ashvaghosha. After meeting him, Kanishka became a follower of Buddhism. Like Ashoka, Kanishka also spread the teachings of Buddha and constructed many Buddhist monasteries, hospitals and rest houses. Historians compare Kanishka with Chandragupta Maurya for his fighting skill and with Ashoka for his belief in Buddhism.

The headless statue of Kanishka

About this time, Jesus Christ spread the idea of one God who cared and loved his people. St. Thomas, one of Christ's disciples is believed to have brought the teachings of Jesus to India. But, one day, while the saint was saying his prayers, he was killed by angry local residents. Today, a beautiful church stands in Chennai, where he is believed to have been killed.

During the reign of the Kushanas, trading grew between Rome and India. The Romans bought spices, Indigo, pearls, jewels and perfumes in India and Indians received gold in return.

Kushana sculpture

Did You Know?
Historians compare Kanishka with Chandragupta Maurya for his fighting skill and with Ashoka for his belief in Buddhism.

 LESSONS TO LEARN...

When people begin to fight amongst themselves,
outsiders take advantage of the situation

The small kingdoms of India fought with each other and reduced each other's strength. As a result of this, the foreign tribes of Kushanas came to India and defeated the Indian kings. If the Indian kings were united they would have been able to stop the attack of the foreigners.

Remember: In unity there is strength.

THE KINGDOMS OF SOUTH INDIA

(Indian History from 200 B.C. - A.D. 300)

The oldest powerful kingdoms of the South were the Cholas, Pandyas and Cheras. The Cholas had a fleet of ships and were experts at naval battle. The Pandyas had a very huge army. The kingdom of Cheras was known for its rich merchants who conducted trade with West Asia by the sea route.

The Satavahanas (225 B.C. - A.D. 225)...

When the Mauryan Empire was breaking up, the Satavahanas were building a strong kingdom in the South. The Satavahana rulers were able and efficient. Being the followers of Hinduism, they ruled according to the principles given in the Hindu law-books, the *Dharmashastras*. The teachings of *Bhagvad Gita* became popular with the people.

Ajanta Caves

Flourish of trade

Some excellent Buddhist buildings were also built during their rule. The most famous of these is at Sanchi. Here an old Ashokan stupa was enlarged to twice its original size. It was surrounded by a railing which had four gateways facing the four main directions. The railings and gateways were carved with scenes from Buddha's life. A large number of Buddhist temples and monasteries too were constructed during this period. Work on the famous Ajanta caves first started at the time of the Satavahana Kings.

The Satavahana kings traded with other kingdoms. Export business flourished and the merchants involved in this business became very rich.

THE GUPTA KINGS

(The Period from A.D. 320 – A.D. 525)

Chandragupta marries Kumaradevi

The first popular Gupta king was Chandragupta (A.D. 320 - A.D. 335). He married Kumaradevi, a princess from the royal family of the Lichchhavis. His marriage made him extend his control over Prayag and Ayodhya. He crowned himself the king of Magadha and took upon the title, of 'Maharajadhiraja' the *great king of kings*. Though he called himself 'Maharajadhiraja', his kingdom was small.

Samudragupta becomes the King (A.D. 335 – A.D. 375)…

After Chandragupta died, his son Samudragupta took over the reigns of the kingdom. Samudragupta was an able ruler and a brave warrior. He fought many wars and conquered many kingdoms. His kingdom extended from Bengal in the East to Delhi in the central West, including central India.

He celebrated his victories by performing *Ashwamedha Yagna* (the ancient horse sacrifice). No one dared to stop the horse Samudragupta had sent and so he proclaimed himself Emperor. Samudragupta's kingdom was large and prosperous. After a gap of several years, India was once again united as one country. The study of science, art and literature flourished. Samudragupta himself was very fond of music and played the veena. Some of his coins show him with a veena in his hands. His rule was gentle and efficient and the country was prosperous.

Samudragupta playing the Veena

The court of Vikramaditya

Did You Know?

Aryabhata, the great astronomer & mathematician, lived during the Gupta period.

The Greatest Gupta King (A.D. 380 – A.D. 414)...

The greatest gupta king was perhaps Samudragupta's son Chandragupta II. He later gave himself the title of *Vikramaditya* (the son of valour). The Gupta empire was at its strongest and largest under the rule of Vikramaditya. He fought battles against the Sakas of Malwa and took over their kingdom.

In spite of his many great conquests, Vikramaditya is better remembered for his contribution in the field of music, art and literature. His court was full of musicians, poets and writers. There were nine people whom he considered the best and called then *Navratnas* (Nine Gems). The great poet and playwriter Kalidasa was one of them whose **Abhigyan Shakuntalam** (Shakuntala) is a very famous play.

Vikramaditya is also remembered for his great sense of justice. The Chinese traveller **Fa Hien** visited India during Vikramaditya's rule and was impressed with him. Fa Hien praised the king and the country in his writings.

Vikramaditya was succeeded by his son Kumaragupta who was later succeeded by Skandagupta. The Gupta kings ruled for almost 200 years. Their rule is known as the 'Golden age of Indian history' as there were great advancements in the field of art, mathematics, music, science and literature.

Aryabhata, the great astronomer and mathematician lived during the Gupta period. He believed that it was really the earth that was moving and not the stars. His belief was that the earth had an invisible axis through its centre and that it rotated on this axis like a ball. The other astronomers of this period believed that the earth was the centre of the solar system, and the sun, the moon and the stars, revolved around the earth. Aryabhata's value for π or 'pi' of 3.1416, is still used today.

Aryabhata, the great astronomer

THE HUNS

(The Period from A.D. 458 – A.D. 558)

During the reign of the Gupta king, Skandagupta, fierce nomads called the Huns came to India. The Huns were from central Asia and were excellent horsemen. They had heard about the wealth of India and decided to invade India.

The Huns could stay on horseback for days together and it is said they could even sleep on horseback! They were good warriors too. Wherever they went, they looted and burned houses, killed people and took away everything they could find.

The Gupta empire breaks up...

The repeated attacks of the Huns reduced the strength of the Gupta kings. Eventually, the Gupta empire broke up into a number of small kingdoms. India, once again was divided into a number of small states. The kings of these small states fought amongst themselves for power and wealth.

The Huns

Did You Know?
The Huns could stay on horseback for days together and it is said they could even sleep on horseback!

THE RULE OF HARSHAVARDHAN

(A.D. 606 – A.D. 647)

King Harshavardhan

Prabhakaravardhan was the king of Thaneshwar. His kingdom was near Kurukshetra (Haryana). He had two sons and one daughter. The sons were Rajyavardhan and Harshavardhan. The daughter was Rajyasri and she was married to the King of Kanauj. After king Prabhakaravardhan died, his eldest son Rajyavardhan became the king.

Rajyavardhan goes to rescue Rajyasri...

Soon, news came from Kanauj that Rajyasri's husband had been killed in a battle by the king of Malwa. Kanauj had been captured and Rajyasri was made a prisoner.

On hearing this news about his sister Rajyasri, Rajyavardhan marched forward to fight the king of Malwa. He fought bravely and defeated the king of Malwa. But when Rajyavardhan was returning to his kingdom, he was killed by another king called Sasanka.

Harshavardhan becomes the King…

After the death of his elder brother, Harshavardhan became the king at the age of 16. After becoming the king, the first thing he did was to attack the king of Malwa. He defeated his enemy and rescued his sister. He also united the kingdoms of Thaneshwar and Kanauj.

Harshavardhan expands his empire…

Harshavardhan realized that the neighbouring kingdoms were a threat to his kingdom. So he decided to conquer them and strengthen his kingdom.

For six years, Harshavardhan fought battle after battle. His elephants and horses were always on the move and his soldiers never removed their armour (war clothes).

He conquered many kingdoms and his empire extended over the whole of North India except Kashmir.

Harshavardhan also tried to extend his kingdom in the South. But there he was defeated by a powerful king Pulakesin II and was forced to go back.

Harshavardhan becomes a Buddhist…

A Chinese traveller Hiuen Tsang came to meet Harshavardhan. Harshavardhan and Hiuen Tsang had many discussions and by the end of it, Harshavardhan became a follower of Buddha.

Hiuen Tsang

Though he became a Buddhist, Harsha continued to pray to Shiva and other Gods of the Hindus. He respected all religions and was a very generous king. Every five years he went to Prayag and gave away to Buddhists, Jains and Hindus, the poor and needy - all he had - Money, Jewels and Clothes. It is said that once he had to borrow an old cloth from his sister to cover himself as he had nothing to wear.

Did You Know?
For six years, Harshavardhan fought battle after battle & his soldiers never removed their armour.

Harshavardhan giving away all
his belongings to the poor

Harshavardhan's Kingdom Prospers...

Harshavardhan's rule was gentle and he was very concerned about the welfare of the people. Like other great kings before him, he also built many hospitals, rest houses and Buddhist monasteries. The standard of education was very high and the students had to pass tough entrance examination to get admission in universities. There was progress in the field of science, medicine, mathematics, philosophy, etc.

We know a lot about Harshavardhan's rule from Hiuen Tsang's book titled Sin-Yu-Ki. This book gives detailed information about the life of the people in his kingdom.

After Harshavardhan's Death...

Harshavardhan died leaving no heir to his kingdom. After his death, his empire soon broke up. Northern India was once again divided into many small and big Kingdoms.

During this period, a new religion **Islam** was becoming popular in Arab. The followers of this religion were called the **Muslims**.

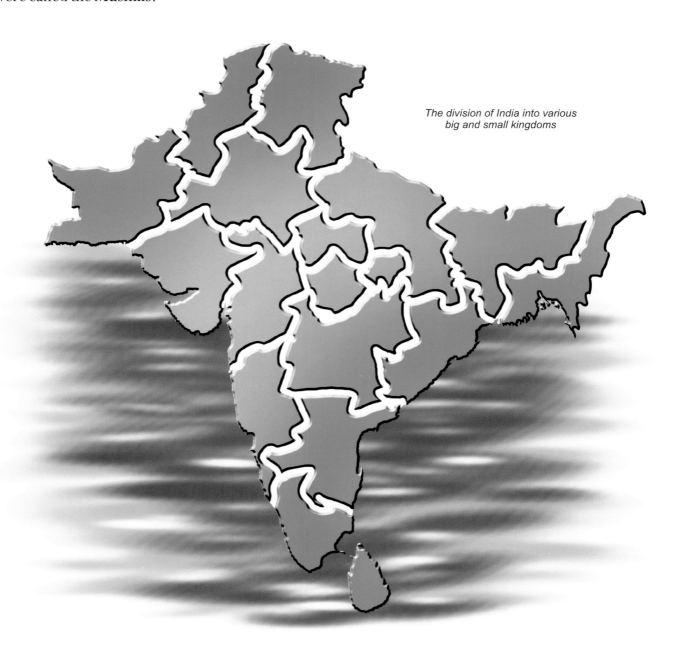

The division of India into various big and small kingdoms

When Harshavardhan was ruling the north (A.D. 606-647), there were three important kingdoms in the south. These were the Chalukyas, the Pallavas and the Pandyas.

The Chalukya Kings...

The greatest Chalukya king was Pulakesin II. He was a very powerful and famous king. Pulakesin II was so powerful that he defeated Harshavardhan and stopped him from entering the south. He was a good ruler and his people respected him. He also defeated the Pallava king Mahendravarman I.

The Pallava Kings...

These were the Tamil kings. In the seventh century, their king was Mahendravarman I. Although he was defeated by Pulakesin II, he was talented in other fields. He was a writer and encouraged many scholars and poets to visit his court.

The son of Mahendravarman became the king after him. His name was Narasimhavarman and he was a better commander than his father. Narasimhavarman defeated Pulakesin II. This reduced the power of the Chalukyas and in A.D. 753, the Rashtrakutas took over from the Chalukyas.

The Rashtrakuta Kings...

The Rashtrakutas became very powerful during the reign of Amoghavarsha. He was a very ambitious king and wanted the Rashtrakutas to be powerful both in the Deccan and the Northern India. So he attempted to control the North by capturing Kanauj.

The three party struggle...

The Pratihara kings ruling in Avanti and the Pala kings ruling in Bengal were also interested in capturing Kanauj. All three of them—the Rashtrakutas, the Palas and the Pratiharas fought continuously with each other for the control of Kanauj. Their continuous war with each other reduced their power and eventually all these kingdoms declined.

The Chola Kings...

The Cholas overthrew the Pallavas in the ninth century. The Cholas became the most powerful kingdom of south India in the eleventh century. This was under the rule of Rajaraj I and later his son Rajendra. They both fought many wars and added new areas to their kingdom.

Rajendra Chola's northern campaign was very similar to Samudragupta's southern campaign which had taken place 700 years earlier. The Chola army marched up to the east coast of India, through Orissa and upto the Ganga river. Rajendra Chola defeated the Pala king of Bengal and called himself '*the Chola who brought the Ganga south*.' The king also built many dams, lakes and canals so that the farmers of his kingdom always had water for their fields. The artisans in the kingdom made beautiful bronze images of Lord Shiva. The great Shiva Temple at Tanjore was built by Rajaraja Chola. The Cholas remained powerful until the thirteenth century after which they declined.

The Shiva Temple at Tanjore

THE RISE OF HINDUISM

In the eighth century, a great man was born in Kerala. His name was Sankara. He studied the holy books of the Hindu religion with great interest and began to think deeply about the religion.

He began asking questions like: 'Who is God? What is the purpose of life? Who am I?'

He developed his ideas and visited places, spreading his teachings. When people would not agree with him, he would argue and make them understand. He preached that God is in everyone and love of God is to be shown in loving one's fellow men.

Eventually, Sankara became **Sankaracharya** (*acharya* means teacher). He wrote many books on philosophy and composed many devotional poems.

Sankaracharya with people

The four maths

Sankaracharya established *four maths* in four corners of India: Badrinath in the north, Puri in the east, Dwarka in the west and Shringeri in the south. Many people visited these places (maths) and they became centres of Hindu learning.

The teachings of Sankaracharya soon spread all over the country and made Hinduism once again the most important religion in India.

THE BRAVE RAJPUTS
(The Period from A.D. 800 - A.D. 1200)

The Rajputs were the descendants of foreign tribes such as the Sakas and Huns. They established powerful kingdoms in northern India in the ninth century. There were four important Rajput families that ruled in the north. These were the Pratiharas, the Chauhans, the Solankis and the Pawars.

The Pratiharas...

The Pratiharas became very powerful during the reign of king Bhoj. He ruled from about A.D. 836 to 882 and was the most famous king of northern India at that time.

Samyukta places the garland of flowers on the clay statue

Bhoj is also remembered for his great interest in literature and for his devotion to God Vishnu. Some of the coins of his period have a picture of the *Varaha* (Boar) incarnation of Vishnu.

The Chauhans...

One of the famous Rajput kings, of whom many stories are told, was Prithiviraj Chauhan. He fell in love, with Samyukta, the beautiful princess of Kanauj. But Samyukta's father Jayachandra hated Prithiviraj and would not let her marry him.

Jayachandra arranged a great *swayamvara* for his daughter to choose her husband. All the princes and kings from far and near were invited. All except Prithiviraj. To make fun of Prithiviraj, a clay statue of his was placed as a doorkeeper at the hall.

All the princes and kings were seated in the hall. Then princess Samyukta came, looked around and walked slowly past the gathering of princes. She lifted the garland of flowers and placed it on the clay statue.

The king and the guests present were shocked on seeing this. Before they could recover from the shock, Prithiviraj himself appeared in the hall. He lifted the princess on his horse and rode away to his kingdom.

The life of the Rajput kings…

The Rajput kings had a lifestyle of their own. They loved war more than anything else. From an early age, the children were taught riding, shooting and other battle skills. Rajput women too were taught to be brave. They also participated in wars if needed. Rajputs preferred to die rather than be dishonoured.

Prithiviraj and Samyukta

Did You Know?
If a Rajput king was killed in war, it was the custom of all the ladies of the court to commit Jauhar, rather than be captured by the enemy.

If a Rajput king was killed in war, the ladies of the court committed suicide by burning themselves alive. They preferred to die rather than be captured by the enemy. This custom was called Jauhar.

The Rajput kings were always fighting with each other to show off their strength. These wars gradually made them weak.

THE INVADERS

(The Period from A.D. 500 – A.D. 1050)

Rise of Islam…

In the year A.D. 570, a great man was born in a little town called Mecca in Arabia. His name was Mohammed. At that time, Arabia was full of warring tribes. Mohammed hated war and wanted the tribes to stop fighting each other. He felt that if the tribes could be united, Arabia would become strong and prosperous.

United Arabs conquer other lands

Mohammed spread his ideas to other people. He taught that there is only one God. All men are equal and there is life after death. We either go to heaven or hell depending on how well we live our lives.

Many people became Mohammed's followers. These people are called Muslims and their religion is Islam. The teachings of Mohammed are compiled in the **Koran** which is a holy book of the Muslims.

United Arabs conquer other lands...

The teachings of Mohammed united the warring tribes and they began conquering other lands. Soon they conquered Syria, Persia, Egypt and the whole of Northern Africa.

In A.D. 712, the Arabs attacked Sind under the leadership of Mohammed Bin Kasim. The Arabs used giant catapults, stone Slings, poisoned arrows and defeated the ruler of Sind. The Arabs conquered Sind but could not go further because of the powerful Rajputs of North India.

Did You Know?
Though Mahmud of Ghazni was a plunderer, he enjoyed the company of poets and scholars.

Mahmud of Ghazni raids India (A.D. 1000 - 1025)

As we have read, the Rajput kings fought among themselves to show off their strength. These battles gradually made them weak.

About this time a Muslim ruler called Mahmud ruled in Ghazni in Afghanistan. He knew of India's great wealth and decided to loot India. He first attacked India in A.D. 1000. Between A.D. 1000 and 1026, he raided India seventeen times and every time the Rajputs failed to stop him. His soldiers were good horsemen and fierce warriors. On each raid he destroyed temples, killed people and carried back treasures of gold and jewels. One of Mahmud's worst attacks was the attack on the famous Somnath temple. This temple was one of the holiest and the richest temples in India. Mahmud along with his soldiers forced his way into the temple and destroyed everything. The priests of the temple begged him to spare the image of shiva but he smashed it to pieces.

Mahmud was very destructive in India but in his own country he was responsible for building a mosque and a large library. Although, he was a plunderer, he enjoyed the company of poets and scholars. The two great writers, Firdausi and AI Beruni lived in his court. Mahmud thought that all the destruction he had done was for the good of Islam.

Mahmud of Ghazni died in A.D. 1030 and the people of northern India felt relieved.

Mahmud of Ghazni destroyed Hindu temples

❧ LESSONS TO LEARN... ☙

Always practice tolerance and respect for other religions

No religion teaches the people to disrespect other religions. Mahmud of Ghazni destroyed temples and hurt the sentiments of the Hindus. He thought that his actions were for the good of his religion Islam. But history only remembers him as a ruthless plunderer.

Muhammad Ghori (end of the 12th century)

After Mahmud of Ghazni, India did not face any foreign invasion for about 160 years. Then in A.D. 1191, another Turkish invader Muhammad Ghori attacked India. He was the ruler of Ghor, a small kingdom in Afghanistan.

Unlike Mahmud of Ghazni, Muhammad Ghori was not only interested in taking back treasures from India. He wanted to conquer North India.

Ghori attacks Prithviraj Chauhan...

Muhammad fought with the Rajput king Prithviraj Chauhan about whom you have already read. The two armies met at Tarain. The Rajput army fought so well that Muhammad was forced to go back to Afghanistan. Although Muhammad went back, he could not forget his defeat. He vowed to avenge his defeat.

The next year, he again attacked Prithviraj with a fine army of 1,20,000 men. Prithviraj was prepared to face him but his father-in-law Jayachandra and the ruler of Gujarat both refused to help him. Jayachandra had not forgiven Prithviraj for forcibly taking away his daughter.

The king of Delhi, Muhammad Ghori

Muhammad Ghori becomes the Sultan (King)...

Muhammad's army met Prithviraj's army on the same battlefield at Tarain. This time Prithviraj was defeated and killed. His queen and her attendants committed Jauhar. Muhammad Ghori won the throne of Delhi in A.D. 1192. Muhammad's campaigns were well organized and when he conquered a territory, he left a general behind to govern it in his absence. Muhammad died in A.D. 1206 and his Governor Qutbuddin Aibak became the king.

 LESSONS TO LEARN...

Learn from your mistakes

We can see that the Indian Kings did not learn anything from the raids of Mahmud of Ghazni and continued fighting with each other. This gave Ghori the opportunity to establish a powerful kingdom in India.

THE DELHI SULTANATE

(The Period from A.D. 1206 - A.D. 1413)

After Muhammad Ghori died in AD 1206, his general Qutbuddin Aibak became the Sultan (King) of Delhi.

The Slave Sultans (A.D. 1206 – 1290)...

Qutbuddin Aibak (A.D. 1206 - 1210) was the first slave king to become the king of Delhi. He ruled for only four years. He destroyed many Hindu temples to collect material for his buildings. He began the construction of the famous Qutab Minar.

After Qutbuddin Aibak, his son Aram Shah (A.D. 1210-1211) became the Sultan. He was later defeated by Iltutmish.

Iltutmish (A.D. 1211-1235) became the king after Aram Shah. He was a good ruler and managed his kingdom well. After Iltutmish died Ruqnuddin Feroz (eldest son Of Iltutmish) was declared Sultan. But Ruqnuddin was murdered after seven months of his rule only. After her brother's death, Raziya started to rule the kingdom. Raziya was a wise and capable ruler. She dressed like a man and rode an elephant.

Raziya (A.D. 1236-1240) was the only Muslim queen to sit on the throne of Delhi. Many of her officers did not like being ruled by a woman. The officers plotted against her and had her killed in A.D. 1240.

Qutub Minar

Raziya Sultan

Did You Know?
Raziya was the only Muslim queen to sit on the throne of Delhi.

The murder of the queen was followed by confusion and more murders. After a number of less important Sultans came Balban, a strong and powerful Sultan. Balban became the king in AD 1266. He ruled with justice and with a firm hand. He had a strong army and controlled the people through fear and force.

The Khilji Sultans (A.D. 1290 – 1320)...

The descendants of Balban were weak. As a result, in A.D. 1290 a new dynasty of Turkish kings called the Khiljis took over the throne of Delhi. The most famous king among the Khiljis was **Alauddin**. He became the king after killing his own uncle Jalauddin. Alauddin was very ambitious. He wanted to become a second Alexander and conquer the world. He began by trying to first conquer the whole of India.

Alauddin fought with the Rajputs and also extended his empire in the south. He sent a large army in the south under his general Malik Kafur. Malik Kafur fought with many kings in the south and collected a large amount of gold from various kingdoms. Malik Kafur even attacked the city of Madurai. No north Indian army had managed to come so far south before. Thus, for a very brief period Alauddin ruled over an empire almost as large as that of king Ashoka.

Allauddin is also known for his reforms in the Delhi Sultanate.

Administrative Reforms: Allauddin introduced a new administrative policy in which he kept administration and religion separate.

Economic Reforms: Allauddin introduced the policy of price control and market control. He did this so that all his subjects (people in his kingdom) could get food items at low prices. He used to also punish the officials who were found taking bribes. He started giving salaries to his soldiers in money. Allauddin also started a new policy of land revenue. He ordered to measure the land and collected land revenue according to the size of the land.

Did You Know?

For a very brief period, Allauddin ruled over an empire almost as large as that of king Ashoka.

The Tughluq Sultans (A.D. 1320 – 1399)...

Allauddin died in A.D. 1316. There was confusion in the kingdom till A.D. 1320 after which a new family of kings called the Tughluqs took control of the throne. One of the important Tughluq rulers was Muhammad-Bin-Tughluq. He was learned and brilliant but some of his ideas to improve his rule failed.

Once he decided to shift his capital from Delhi to far off Devagiri (near Aurangabad). He renamed it Daulatabad and thought it to be a better place for controlling the Deccan. All men, women and children were ordered to move to the new capital. However, this plan failed as Daulatabad was too far from northern Indian and the Sultan could not keep a watch on the northern frontiers. Muhammad returned to Delhi and Delhi again became the capital. However, the southern kingdoms saw this as a sign of weakness on the part of the Tughluq king. Soon after, two independent kingdoms arose in the Deccan and the Tughluqs now had no say in the matters of the Deccan.

Muhammad-bin-Tughluq shifts his capital

Another experiment that Muhammad tried also failed. He decided to have copper coins instead of gold and silver coins. The copper coins were stamped to show their value in gold and silver. But the minting of these coins was not properly controlled. Everyone began making their own copper coins. Gold and silver disappeared and there were so many copper coins that they were worth nothing. The Sultan had to change his order.

Muhammad-Bin-Tughluq lost the support of his people because of his bad decision. Moreover, he lost the support of his nobles and the *ulema*. The *ulemas* were the scholars of Islamic learning who were generally orthodox in their outlook. Some of Muhammad's policies could have been successful if he was better advised and supported by the *ulema* and the nobles.

LESSONS TO LEARN...

Think before you act
The decisions of Muhammad-Bin-Tughluq resulted in his downfall. He carried out his decisions without thinking about the results.

The Break up of the Delhi Sultanate...

After Muhammad-Bin-Tughluq, his cousin Firoz Shah (A.D. 1351-1388) took over the throne. Firoz realized that one of the reasons for Muhammad's failure was that he did not have the support of the *ulemas* and the nobles, So to win their support, Firoz gave them grants of revenue. He allowed the orthodox *ulema* to influence state policy in certain matters. Firoz was not only less tolerant of non-Muslims but also of those Muslims who were not orthodox. Although, Firoz improved his relationships with the powerful group (the *ulemas* and the nobles), but at the same time the power of the Sultan (his power) decreased. The governors in certain provinces of his empire rebelled against him. Firoz tried to bring his empire under control but was not successful. The death of Firoz Shah was followed by a civil war amongst his descendants. The governors of many provinces broke away and became independent kings. By the end of the 14th century, only a small area around Delhi remained in the hands of the Tughluq Sultans.

The final blow to the Tughluq empire came from Timur, a fierce Mongol, who came from Samarkand in central Asia. He attacked Delhi with an army of 90,000 horsemen. The weak Tughluq rulers could not defend themselves against Timur's army. For five days, Timur looted and killed and then returned to Samarkand with what he had collected. When Timur returned to Samarkand, he had left behind one of his officers, Khizr Khan.

The Tughluq dynasty ended in A.D. 1413. Khizr Khan proclaimed himself Sultan of Delhi and founded the Sayyad dynasty which ruled Delhi for 37 years. This was followed by an Afghan dynasty, the Lodhis. But the kingdom which they ruled did not extend much beyond Delhi.

Destruction by Timur

LIFE OF THE PEOPLE
(13th Century to 16th Century)

The Hindus and the Muslims living together

The Muslims and the Hindus...

The Muslims who came to India brought with them a different way of life. Many Muslims settled in India and made India their home. They mixed with the Hindus and learnt some of their customs. Some Hindus were forced by the Sultan to become Muslims and accept Islam as their religion. Some other, mostly poor, converted to Islam as the converts were offered food and shelter. Despite the powers of the Sultan and the attractions of a new religion, most Hindus did not change their religion.

Start of a new language, Urdu...

The language of the Muslims was Arabic. Most of the Hindus in and around Delhi spoke Hindi. When the Hindus and Muslims started mixing with each other, a new language called **Urdu** was born. It had Hindi grammar and Arabic words.

Changes in Culture...

Many changes took place in the areas of food, clothes and medicine. New style of clothes such as *pyjama*, *kaftan* and *salwar kameez* became popular. A new form of dance called Kathak emerged. In this the dancer wore Persian clothes but acted out Hindi stories. During this period, the great poet *Amir Khushro* combined the Indian Veena with the Persian Tanpura to make a new instrument, the *Sitar*. He also altered the South Indian drum to *Tabla*.

Did You Know?
When battles were being fought, the farmers were seen doing their work in the fields as they never cared who won or who lost.

Life of Poor People...

The life of the poor people remained the same. The changes introduced with the coming of the Turks and Afghans were limited to the upper classes. The poor people were not concerned about who ruled the country as they believed that their condition would remain the same. Often when battles were being fought, the farmers were seen doing their work in the fields as they never cared who won or who lost! The caste system had become even more rigid and the upper castes treated the lower castes badly.

Kathak

Tabla

Sitar

THE NEW RELIGIOUS GROUPS
(13th Century to 16th Century)

The Sufis...

In the eleventh century, there were some Muslim Saints who came to India along with the Turkish invaders. These Muslim saints lived a simple life and mixed freely with the Hindu saints and gurus. These were called the *Sufis*. The Sufis believed that God was present everywhere. Through love and devotion one can come nearer to God. They also believed in the equality of all men. The Sufis said that even the poor people can come nearer to God without the help of priests and religious ceremonies. All they need is a heart full of love and devotion. These ideas became very popular with the Indian people and soon the *Sufis* had many Indian followers.

One of the popular *Sufi* saints was Muin-ud-din Chishti. He believed that playing or singing beautiful music was almost like being in the presence of God. Chishti's followers held gatherings where some of the finest music could be heard. The *qawwali* was a popular form of singing at these gatherings.

The Bhakti Movement...

Besides the Sufis, there was another religious movement which became very popular during this period. This was the *Bhakti* Movement. *Bhakti* simply means devotion or love.

Qawwali, the musical form of worship

Did You Know?
One of the famous bhaktas was a princess, called Mirabai. She was married into the royal family of Mewar, but fine clothes, precious jewels and all the comforts of the palace meant nothing to her. Her thoughts were only for Lord Krishna whom she loved. She composed beautiful songs in his honour and spent her time singing them.

The bhaktas

The *Bhakti* movement was founded by Basava and most of the *Bhakti* saints were from the non-brahmin castes. The *Bhakti* saints also taught that the relationship between man and God was based on true love and devotion. In Benaras, there was a very popular Bhakti saint. His name was Kabir. Kabir was the son of a Brahmin (Hindu) widow. His mother had abandoned him and he was brought up by a Muslim weaver.

Kabir taught that God is one, whether the Hindus worship him as Ram or the Muslims worship him as *Allah*. Religious ceremonies and fasting is of no use if we do not have true devotion to God. Many Hindus and Muslims became Kabir's followers. There is a story that when Kabir died, the Hindus wanted to burn his body while the Muslims wanted to bury it. There was a quarrel and when the sheet over his dead body was removed, there was just a heap of rose petals.

Both the *Sufi* and *Bhakti* movements greatly influenced the ideas of the people and brought the Hindus and Muslims closer.

Another great saint, *Guru Nanak* was born in 1469. He founded the *Sikh* religion. (See page 137 for detailed information).

Kabir with both Hindus and Muslims

BABAR - THE WARRIOR

(The Founder of the Mughal Dynasty)
(A.D. 1526 – A.D. 1530)

Portrait of Babar

Did You Know?
The Babar Nama recounts almost 40 years of Babar's adventures, opinions and ideas.

The Lodhi Kings...

At the beginning of the 16th century, the Lodhi kings were ruling the Delhi Sultanate. But the Delhi sultanate had become small. It had broken into many parts and these parts had established themselves as small independent kingdoms. Thus, the kingdom of the Lodhis did not extend much beyond Delhi. The rulers of these small kingdoms were fighting among themselves and reduced each others' strength.

Babar was the king of Kabul (in Afghanistan) who saw this as an opportunity to attack India. Like his ancestor Timur, he too wanted to loot India.

The First Battle of Panipat…

In 1526, Babar fought with Ibrahim Lodhi on the famous plain of Panipat. The Lodhi army was defeated and this battle is known as the **First Battle of Panipat**. Babar's army used modern weapons like guns and cannons and his soldiers were well trained. Babar himself was a good general and arranged his soldiers in such a way that they could be easily moved from one part of the battle to another. In addition to this, Babar was also helped by the Rajput prince Rana Sanga of Mewar and some Afghan administrators (officers). They wanted to get rid of the Lodhis and thus helped Babar to defeat the Lodhis.

The Rajput prince and the Afghan administrators expected Babar to return to Kabul after defeating Ibrahim Lodhi. But after the victory, Babar not only took his share of the wealth but also decided to stay in India. So he occupied Delhi and Agra.

Now, Rana Sanga and the Afghan officers turned against him. Rana Sanga attacked Babar with a huge army in 1527. But Babar's army used modern weapons like guns and his soldiers were excellent horsemen. As a result, the Rajput prince was defeated. Later, Babar fought with the Afghan officers as well and defeated them too.

Babar, the learned King…

Babar was not only a great general and a warrior but also a very learned man. He was a poet and also a writer.

The first battle of Panipat

He wrote down whatever he saw and felt. His writings are called the *Babar Nama* and are a valuable source of history. Babar was very fond of natural beauty, mountains, trees, flowers and animals. This is why he was always keen to make gardens in all the palaces he lived.

Babar died in 1530 and at this time his kingdom included the whole of Punjab, Delhi and the Ganga plain as far as Bihar.

LESSONS TO LEARN...

Never trust a powerful enemy

The Rajput prince Rana Sanga and the Afghan chiefs plotted with Babar to get rid of Ibrahim Lodhi. They believed that after defeating the Lodhis, Babar would return to Afghanistan and they would occupy Delhi. But Babar had other plans. He established his kingdom in India and occupied the throne of Delhi. Thus, the plan of Rana Sanga and Afghan chiefs failed.

HUMAYUN - THE DREAMER

(A.D. 1530 – A.D. 1540 AND A.D. 1555 – A.D. 1556)

Portrait of Humayun

After Babar died in 1530, his son Humayun inherited the kingdom. Although Humayun inherited a vast kingdom, it was not safe. It was surrounded by rulers who wanted the Mughals to leave India. The most dangerous enemy of Humayun was king Bahadur Shah of Gujarat.

Humayun attacks Bahadur Shah...

Humayun attacked Bahadur Shah and occupied the forts of Mandu and Champaner. Bahadur Shah had to run away from his kingdom to save his life. At this time, Humayun was only 23 years old but he was a brave and an experienced commander. But he also had a serious drawback.

He liked to enjoy himself and put pleasure before work. Instead of making his kingdom strong and safe, he wasted all his time in drinking and enjoying himself. About this time, an Afghan ruler Sher Shah Suri decided to attack the Mughal king.

Sher Shah Suri...

Sher Shah's real name was Farid Shah. He was given the name 'Sher' after he killed a tiger. Sher Shah had inherited a small estate from his father. Sher was ambitious and his ambition led him to acquire more and more land and build a strong army. He became an independent king. He decided to attack Humayun and conquer Delhi.

Sher Shah defeats Humayun...

The battle between Sher Shah and Humayun went on for 2 years. In 1540, Humayun was finally defeated and Sher Shah became the king

The birth of Akbar...

After being defeated, Humayun moved from one place to another for shelter. For the next 15 years, he was homeless. During this period, Humayun married a 14 year old girl, Hamida.

Sher shah defeats Humayun in battle

She later gave birth to a baby boy whom they named Akbar. Humayun with his wife and son went to Persia where the king of Persia gave them shelter.

The death of Sher Shah...

Sher Shah who had defeated Humayun ruled for only 5 years. He was a good ruler and his people were happy with him. He built many roads, wells and rest houses. Although he was a Muslim, he did not ill-treat the followers of other religions. Sher Shah was killed in 1545 in a battle at Kalinjar. After him, his son Islam Shah ruled for 9 years.

Humayun becomes the king again...

Humayun with the help of the Shah (king) of Persia recaptured the throne and became the king in 1555. Six months later, one morning while he was coming down the staircase, he fell down and was seriously hurt. He died soon after.

LESSONS TO LEARN...

Put work before pleasure

Although Humayun was a good general, he was not a successful king as he always put pleasure before work. Instead of making his empire strong and looking after his people, he spent all his time in enjoying himself. He neglected his duties and had to suffer for it. He spent 15 years of his life wandering homeless.

AKBAR - THE GREAT

(A.D. 1556 - A.D. 1605)

Portrait of Akbar

After Humayun died in 1556, his son Akbar was made the king. But at this time, Akbar was only 13 years old and managing the kingdom was a big responsibility for a young boy. So, his guardian Bairam Khan looked after the matters of the kingdom.

Himu occupies Delhi…

During this time, the nephews of Sher Shah, Adil and Sikandar, decided to conquer Delhi. They sent an army under the leadership of their Hindu general Himu. Himu along with his army occupied Delhi.

The Second Battle of Panipat…

Bairam Khan along with the Mughal army met Himu's army on the same battlefield of Panipat where Babar had defeated Ibrahim Lodhi. This battle was fought in 1556 and known as the *second battle of Panipat*. The battlefield of Panipat again proved to be lucky for the Mughals as Himu was defeated and killed in the battle. Sher Shah's nephews Sikandar and Adil were also defeated at Agra. The Mughals reoccupied Delhi and Agra which they had lost.

Akbar manages the Kingdom…

For the next four years, the matters of the kingdom were managed by Bairam Khan. Akbar spent all his time playing polo, hunting and riding fierce animals. In 1560, when Akbar turned 18, he decided to take charge of his kingdom. Bairam Khan was released from his duties.

Akbar, the great conqueror…

Akbar wanted to build a large empire so he fought several battles and conquered many territories. Akbar wanted to have friendly relationship with the Rajputs.

King Akbar's court

He did this by marrying several Rajput princesses. His policy of friendship and marriage alliance with the Rajputs made his position stronger. But there were some Rajputs who opposed him. One of them was Rana Pratap. Akbar fought against these Rajputs and captured the forts of Ranthambor and Chittor.

Did You Know?
In the second battle of Panipat, it first appeared that Himu would win. But, then suddenly, he was hit by an arrow in the eye and fell unconscious.

The birth of Salim...

By the time Akbar was 26 years old, he had many wives and daughters but no son. Akbar was upset and he visited a Muslim saint named Salim Chishti who promised him 3 sons. The promise came true and his eldest son was born in 1569. Akbar named his son Salim who became the King after Akbar. In honour of the saint, Akbar built a new city called Fatehpur Sikri in 1571 and made it his capital.

Did You Know?
It is said that Akbar could barely sign his name but was always surrounded by scholars, artists and poets.

The city of Fatehpur Sikri

Akbar, the popular king...

Akbar was a follower of Islam but he respected all religions. The people in his kingdom were free to follow any religion and people of all religions were considered equal. This policy made Akbar extremely popular with people of all religions. Akbar's policies united the Hindus and Muslims and gave the Indian people a feeling of unity. They felt as though they were members of one large family. The Indian people not only accepted the Mughals but also started respecting and loving them.

Akbar and his Nine Gems...

Akbar could not read or write well but he enjoyed the company of scholars. In his court, there were nine such people whom he was particularly fond of. He called them his *Navaratnas* or nine gems. They included Abu Fazl, his chief minister, Faizi, the poet who translated the Bhagvad Gita into Persian, Tansen, the great musician and the clever Birbal.

Some of Akbar's Navaratans

JAHANGIR - THE NATURE LOVER
(A.D. 1605 - A.D. 1627)

Salim became the king in 1605 after his father, Akbar, died. He took charge of the kingdom and gave himself the title of *Jahangir* or 'siezer of the world'.

Jahangir, the king...

Jahangir was a good ruler and is remembered for his sense of justice. He made sure that everyone, rich or poor, weak or strong got full justice. Jahangir shared his father Akbar's interest in religion but never studied the problems of religion as deeply as his father. He also did not have his father's sharp mind. But he was well read and a good writer.

Jahangir marries Nur Jahan...

In 1611, Jahangir married Mehrunisa, the beautiful daughter of a Persian nobleman (officer). He called her *Nur Jahan* which means the light of the world. Nur Jahan was not only very beautiful, she was also very intelligent and educated. Jahangir loved her very much and gave her everything she asked for. Her father and brother were given the highest post in the Mughal government.

Nur Jahan becomes the real ruler...

Jahangir fell ill for a long period and during this time Nur Jahan looked after the matters of the kingdom. She managed the kingdom well and even after Jahangir recovered, he still took Nur Jahan's advice in important matters. Many important decisions were taken by Nur Jahan. She became so important that her name appeared along with Jahangir's name on the coins and Nur Jahan became the real ruler.

Did You Know?
It was during Jahangir's reign that the British made their first attempts to send merchants and ships to India for trade.

Sketch of Nur Jahan

The British meet Jahangir...

It was during Jahangir's reign that the British made their first attempts to send merchants and ships to India for trade. Two British ambassadors, Captain Hawkins and Sir Thomas Roe came to India to meet the emperor. When they visited the court, Jahangir's daughter was very ill. Captain Hawkins had some idea about medicine and offered to treat her. The treatment worked and Jahangir's daughter recovered. Jahangir was very happy.

"I am very happy with you, Hawkins. Name what you want," said Jahangir.

"Your majesty, I want you to give me permission to let my country trade with yours," replied Hawkins. Jahangir gave the permission. The British set up factories in Surat and Broach. Jahangir had no idea that one day these traders would become the rulers of India.

The death of Jahangir...

Jahangir strengthened the Mughal empire and continued having friendly relations with the Rajputs. Jahangir loved nature and his love of nature made him visit Kashmir many times. In 1627, while he was returning from one of his holidays in Kashmir, he fell ill and died. His son Shah Jahan took over the reigns of the Mughal empire.

SHAH JAHAN - THE BUILDER
(A.D. 1627 - A.D. 1658)

Portrait of Shah Jahan

Shah Jahan became the king in 1628. He wanted to conquer more territories and strengthen the Mughal empire. He conquered Ahamadnagar in 1633. Shah Jahan also sent his army in the south and conquered territories. But in the north he did not have much success. He lost Kandhar to the Persians.

Shah Jahan, the emperor who built the Taj Mahal...

Shah Jahan is remembered as the emperor who built the Taj Mahal in Agra and the Red Fort and Jama Masjid in Delhi.

The Taj Mahal was built by Shah Jahan in memory of his wife, Arjumand Bano Begum. Shah Jahan loved her very much and called her Mumtaz Mahal. Twenty thousand labourers worked for twenty two years to build the Taj Mahal. A huge amount of money and time was spent in building the Taj Mahal. The Taj Mahal is among the few wonders of the world because of its beauty and elegance. It is regarded as the world's famous monument of love.

Portrait of Mumtaz Mahal

Shah Jahan also built a beautiful throne for himself. It was a golden, jewel studded throne which cost over a crore rupees. It had two peacocks, blazing with precious stones of many colours. It was called the Peacock throne.

Did You Know?
Shah Jahan had cut off the hands of the workers after the completion of Taj Mahal so that no one would be able to build such a marvelous monument again.

Taj Mahal

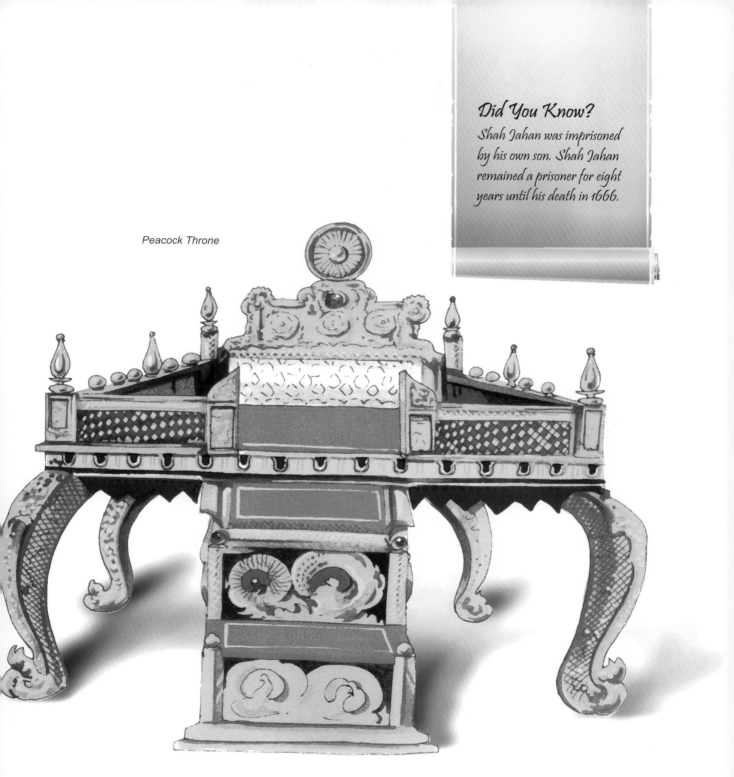

Peacock Throne

Did You Know?
Shah Jahan was imprisoned by his own son. Shah Jahan remained a prisoner for eight years until his death in 1666.

Shah Jahan becomes a prisoner...

When Shah Jahan became old and weak, his four sons began to fight among themselves for the throne. Shah Jahan wanted his eldest son Dara Shikoh to be the king. But the most capable was his third son Aurangzeb.

One day, Aurangzeb defeated his brothers and put his old father in the prison. Aurangzeb crowned himself the king. Shah Jahan remained a prisoner for eight years until his death in 1666 at the age of 74. During all these years, Aurangzeb never met his father.

AURANGZEB - THE CRUEL
(A.D. 1658 – A.D. 1707)

Portrait of Aurangzeb

Aurangzeb came to the throne in 1658 after defeating all his brothers. He was a good warrior and an excellent general. He was also extremely hard-working and did not sleep for more than 2 hours a day.

The problems in the kingdom...

Aurangzeb ruled for almost 50 years. But his reign was full of troubles. The Mughal empire was now larger than ever before. Aurangzeb ruled over nearly the whole of India. But it was difficult to control such a large empire. Many people in different parts of the kingdom were fighting to establish their independent kingdoms. Aurangzeb spent most of his time and money in fighting these people.

The enemies of Aurangzeb…

Aurangzeb gave up the path of friendship and marriage alliance with the Rajputs which Akbar had started. In 1678, when the Rajput king Jaswant Singh of Marwar died, Aurangzeb tried to take over his kingdom.

He brought Jaswant Singh's widow and young son to Delhi. This he did to make sure that the young prince would never demand his father's kingdom when he grew up.

But some loyal and brave followers of Jaswant Singh rescued them from Aurangzeb. The Rajputs fought bravely against the Mughals and in the end Aurangzeb was forced to give them some independence. Aurangzeb also fought with the Sikhs in the north and the Marathas in the Deccan (about whom you will read later).

Aurangzeb, the religious king…

Even as a young man, Aurangzeb was a very religious person. He lived his life strictly according to the rules of Islam. He lived a simple life. Unlike other Mughal rulers, he was not fond of wine, music and luxury. Aurangzeb banned music in his court and removed all poets, artisans and scholars from his court.

Did You Know?
Aurangzeb was extremely hard working & did not sleep for more than 2 hours a day. He was also not fond of wine, music & luxury.

Mughal soldiers ill treating Hindus

Aurangzeb, the Cruel King...

Aurangzeb had fixed religious views and believed that only the religion Islam should be followed by all people in his kingdom. He re-imposed *Jazia* (extra tax) on Hindu people and destroyed Hindu temples. Thus, because of his ill-treatment and cruelty to the Hindus, he lost their love and respect which Akbar had won for the Mughals.

Aurangzeb died in 1707. He was the last important Mughal king. After his death, the Mughal empire soon broke up.

LESSONS TO LEARN...

Follow the path of friendship and kindness

The unfriendly and cruel policies of Aurangzeb resulted in the decline of the Mughal empire after his death.

SHIVAJI - THE BRAVE MARATHA

(A.D. 1627 - A.D. 1680)

During the time when Aurangzeb ruled, the Mughal empire included the whole of north India, central India and a part of south India. About this time, there was a powerful Maratha leader in the Deccan, Shivaji.

The Brave Shivaji...

Shivaji was born in 1627. His father Shahji was an officer in the army of the Sultan of Ahmadnagar. Since Shahji had to be away from home most of the time, Shivaji was brought up by his mother Jijabai. Jijabai was a very brave and a religious woman. She told Shivaji the stories of Ramayana and Mahabharata and sang songs about the heroic deeds of their heroes. She always encouraged Shivaji to be brave.

Shivaji, the great Maratha

119

DadaJi Kond Dev was Shivaji's guardian and teacher. He taught Shivaji how to ride, shoot and become a leader. Shivaji's companions were tough shepherd boys of the hills. With them, he rode the wildest horses. Soon, Shivaji had a few loyal followers. Shivaji was ambitious and decided to set up an independent kingdom. He captured a few forts with his small group of soldiers. But in doing this he spent all his money and had nothing left to pay his soldiers.

Then, one day, an opportunity presented itself. Some treasure was being taken from Kalyan to Bijapur. Shivaji attacked the soldiers carrying the treasure and carried off all the treasure to his fort.

Shivaji kills Afzal Khan

Afzal Khan plans to kill Shivaji...

When the Sultan of Bijapur came to know of this, he became very furious. He sent Afzal Khan, one of his most capable generals, to kill Shivaji.

Afzal Khan made a wicked plan to kill Shivaji. He sent a Brahmin named Krishnaji to meet Shivaji. Krishnaji said, "Shivaji, you and Afzal should meet alone and settle things without fighting." But Shivaji was very clever and did not fall for this trick. He managed to make Krishnaji confess that Afzal wanted to kill him. Shivaji agreed to meet Afzal alone, but prepared himself for the meeting.

Shivaji kills Afzal Khan...

Shivaji put on a steel helmet and covered it carefully with his turban. He wore a suit of steel (armour) underneath his clothes. He also hid a dagger up his sleeve and held a row of sharp steel claws in the palm of his left hand.

"Let's become friends and stop fighting," said Afzal Khan when he met Shivaji. Afzal saw that Shivaji did not have a sword. He himself had his sword at his side. At first, it appeared that the two were embracing but actually Afzal Khan had held Shivaji's neck in a wrestler's grip with his left hand and struck him with his sword. But Shivaji was saved because of his steel suit. At the same time Shivaji had plunged the dagger into Afzal's back and torn open his belly with the steel claws.

Afzal was killed and Shivaji became the ruler of the whole of Konkan region.

Escape from the prison

Aurangzeb sends Jai Singh...

The Mughal emperor Aurangzeb wanted to crush Shivaji's rising power. So he sent his most powerful general Jai Singh to conquer Shivaji's kingdom. Within three months, Jai Singh captured many of Shivaji's forts. Shivaji was forced to accept Aurangzeb as the emperor. He was asked to attend the Mughal court as the other defeated rulers.

Aurangzeb insults Shivaji...

At the Mughal court, Shivaji was offered a seat with people much below his rank. Shivaji felt insulted and walked out of the court. Aurangzeb ordered Shivaji to be imprisoned. But Shivaji was not the one to give up hope and remain imprisoned.

He made a clever plan to escape from prison. He declared that he wanted to please God by sending fruits and sweetmeats to Brahmins and holy men. Aurangzeb consented to this seemingly harmless request. So, one fine day, Shivaji asked for huge baskets. They were going to fill these baskets with sweetmeats and fruits. But there was something else also! In one of the large baskets of fruits, Shivaji hid himself and managed to escape from prison. Once in the city, he disguised himself as a *sanyasi* or travelling monk. Shivaji returned to the Deccan and the joy of the Maratha people knew no bounds.

Shivaji attacks the Mughals...

After reaching the Deccan, he started building up his army. By 1670, he recaptured many of the forts that he had lost to the Mughals.

Although Shivaji's army was small and ill equipped as compared to the Mughal army, still he was successful. This was because he used unique methods of war. He practiced what was called as **Guerilla warfare**. In this, the Maratha soldiers would suddenly attack the Mughal army, throw everything into confusion and then go back and hide. By the time the Mughals recaptured a fort, Shivaji would be several kilometers away, storming another fort. The slow moving Mughals could not keep pace with Shivaji's swift horsemen.

Guerilla warfare

Ghorpad

Shivaji used the ghorpad, a large hill lizard to climb the smooth and straight surfaces of the forts. A rope ladder would be tied around the ghorpad and the creature would dart up the steep wall of the fort. Then a Maratha would climb up the ladder and fix it to the wall so that the soldiers could climb.

Shivaji, the popular Hero...

Shivaji was crowned the king of the Marathas in 1674. He conquered many kingdoms in the South. When he died in 1680, at the age of 53, he was the ruler of a large, independent state. Shivaji was a brave, fearless warrior and remains one of India's most popular heroes.

LESSONS TO LEARN...

Success comes to those who fight hard against failure

THE FALL OF THE MUGHAL EMPIRE
(The Period from A.D. 1707 - A.D. 1739)

After Aurangzeb's death, prince Mauzzam became the king. He was over 60 years of age and died soon. Jahadar Shah succeeded him who was later overthrown by Farrukhsiyar. In 1719, Farrukhsiyar was killed and Muhammad Shah came to the throne.

The Break-up of the empire...

Muhammad Shah was not a good ruler and always kept himself surrounded by musicians and dancers. He spent all his time in drinking and enjoying himself and came to be known as Muhammad Shah *Rangila* (or the colourful). Seeing weakness of the Mughal emperor, various officers in different parts of the empire broke away from the empire. They established their independent kingdoms. Soon, the Mughal empire which once included almost the whole of India, shrank to only the areas surrounding Delhi.

The invasion of Nadir Shah...

The power of the Mughal emperor was further weakened by the attacks of the Persian ruler, Nadir Shah. Nadir Shah carried away huge amount of gold, jewels and other treasures from India to his country. He also killed many people and destroyed many beautiful buildings in India. The invasion of Nadir Shah was a deathblow to the Mughal empire.

Attack of Nadir Shah

THE MARATHAS BECOME STRONGER
(A.D. 1689 - A.D. 1761)

Balaji Baji Rao

After Shivaji's death, his son Shambhuji became the king. But Shambhuji was not a good ruler. He just believed in enjoying himself. In 1689, he was captured by a small Mughal army and was killed. Shambhuji's son Shahu was taken as a prisoner by Aurangzeb. But the Marathas did not give up. Shambhuji's brother Rajaram took over the throne. When Rajaram died in A.D. 1700, his widow Tarabai continued to fight the Mughals.

Shahu becomes the king...

After Aurangzeb's death in 1707, Shahu was sent back to Maharashtra. This was the trick of the Mughals to divide the Marathas and weaken them. Shahu claimed his right to the throne but his aunt Tarabai strongly objected.

The Mughal trick seemed to work for a while but soon Shahu gained control of the Maratha kingdom and became the king in 1708. During his fight to become the king, he was helped by a clever brahmin called Balaji Vishwanath. As a reward for his help, Balaji was appointed the Peshwa (chief minister).

The Peshwas...

Gradually, the Peshwa became the most important officer in the kingdom and soon the Peshwa became even more important than the king himself. After Balaji's death, his son Baji Rao I became the Peshwa. The post of the Peshwa became hereditary.

Baji Rao, the great Maratha…

After Shivaji, Baji Rao I was the greatest Maratha ruler. He was a brilliant commander and expanded the Maratha kingdom. By 1738, the Maratha kingdom included the whole of central India between the Narmada and Chambal. The Maratha kingdom was transformed from a small state to a large empire.

Balaji Baji Rao…

Balaji Baji Rao took over the post from his father in 1740. After nine years when Shahu died, his son Rajaram became the king. Rajaram was a weak ruler. In 1750, Balaji took control of the kingdom and put Rajaram in prison.

The Third Battle of Panipat…

The Afghan ruler Ahmad Shah Abdali fought with the Marathas and conquered Pubjab. Balaji Baji Rao was determined to avenge this defeat. The two armies met at Panipat on 14th January 1761. This battle is known as the *third battle of Panipat*. The Maratha army was badly defeated and lost over one lac soldiers. This was a shock from which the Marathas could not recover. Balaji himself died of grief six months later.

The Break up of the Maratha kingdom…

After the death of Balaji Baji Rao, the Maratha chiefs began to fight among themselves. The Maratha kingdom broke up into 5 independent states — Baroda, Indore, Gwalior, Nagpur and Poona.

Third battle of Panipat

THE BRITISH IN INDIA

(In the 17th Century)

The British Traders

Traders from Europe…

The Arabs had been trading with India for centuries, using the sea route across the Arabian sea. In 1498, a Portuguese sailor named Vasco da Gama sailed round Africa and reached Calicut (Kozhikode) on India's west coast. The discovery of this sea route made the Portuguese ships sail regularly to India.

The Portuguese started trading with India and made huge profits. They decided to chase away the Arabs and take over the entire trade. The Portuguese had a powerful fleet of ships. They captured an important port, Goa.

The other traders from Europe had seen what the Portuguese had done and decided to follow in their footsteps. The traders from Holland (Dutch), England (British) and France (French) came and captured some areas of the Portuguese.

The British Traders...

In 1600, a small group of merchants formed a company called the East India company. Their first ships landed at Surat.

In 1615, the English obtained permission from the Mughal emperor Jahangir to establish trading posts in several towns. The English traders built forts and kept soldiers and guns to protect themselves. Eventually, most of trade passed into the hands of the British. The British had a brilliant leader Robert Clive. The French also continued setting up trading centres. They were led by a very capable leader Dupleix.

The Indian rulers continued fighting with each other for power and wealth. The English and the French took advantage of this situation. They supported Indian kings and even lent their soldiers whenever fighting broke out between two Indian rulers.

The British meeting the traitor Mir Jaffar

Traders become Rulers...

By 1740, the Mughal emperor had become very weak and had power only over a small area around Delhi. The power of the British and the French had increased. Every time a war broke out between two Indian kings, the British and the French took sides and helped them.

Chanda Sahib and Muhammad Ali, two powerful nobles, both wanted the throne of Arcot in the south. Chanda Sahib approached the French for help and Muhammad Ali approached the British. In the war, Chanda Sahib was killed and Muhammad Ali became the king. But he was only a puppet king. The British made him do exactly what they wanted.

The British also fought with Siraj-ud-daulah, the Nawab (king) of Bengal. Siraj-ud-daulah did not like the British. So the British decided to overthrow the Nawab and put their puppet king on the throne. They chose Mir Jaffar, a wicked uncle of Siraj-ud-daulah for this purpose.

131

Siraj-ud-daulah had a well equipped huge army of about 50,000 soldiers. The British army was ill prepared and much smaller in number (about 3,000 soldiers). The two armies met on the field of Plassey in 1757. But a large section of the Nawab's army was led by the traitor Mir Jaffar. That section of the army did not fight at all. By evening, Siraj-ub-daulah was defeated. The next day, Mir Jaffar was made the new Nawab of Bengal. But he was totally controlled by the British. He was a ruler only in name.

After this victory, the British became more powerful. They received a lot of wealth and jewels and gradually took over the right to collect taxes and administer civil justice in Bengal. In the meantime, the battle of Panipat between the Afghan, Ahmad Shah Abdali and the Marathas had taken place. This is known as the third battle of Panipat and the Marathas were completely crushed. This helped the British indirectly as this battle not only shattered the Marathas but also Abdali's presence in the north greatly weakened the Mughal's authority.

Did You Know?
The British won the Battle of Plassey with a force of 3,000 soldiers even though they were opposed by the Nawab's army of 50,000 soldiers.

The British siding with one Indian king against the other

British rule brought a lot of misery to the people of Bengal and especially to the weavers of cotton and silk. The British exploited them and forced them to sell their produce at very low prices.

Robert Clive became the first governor of Bengal. In 1767, when he left India, the British who had initially come as traders, had now become the rulers of a large and prosperous region in India.

Robert Clive, the first Governor of Bengal

LESSONS TO LEARN...

When two people quarrel - a third person gains

The Indian kings were greedy and suspicious of each other and the British took advantage of this. They encouraged the Indian kings to fight with each other. These fights reduced their strength and gradually the British became the rulers of India.

TIPU SULTAN
(A.D. 1782 – A.D. 1799)

The Brave King, Hyder Ali...

During the time when the British were becoming powerful in India, the state of Mysore (in south India) was ruled by a brave king, Hyder Ali. Hyder Ali was ambitious and extended his power in southern India. In 1776, he attacked the kingdom of Malabar and fought with the British. The British signed a treaty by which they agreed to help Hyder Ali if he was attacked by any other ruler.

Hyder Ali becomes angry with the British...

Two year later, the Marathas attacked Hyder Ali. But the British did not help him. This made Hyder Ali very angry with the British. In 1780, he captured Arcot. The British governor general Warren Hastings sent an army from Bengal. Hyder Ali fought bravely but was defeated in several battles. In 1782, he died leaving his son Tipu to continue the war.

Tipu Sultan, the Great Warrior...

After Hyder Ali's death, the British thought that they had got rid of a very dangerous enemy. But soon they realized that the new ruler of Mysore, Tipu Sultan, was even more dangerous. The British realized the power of Tipu Sultan and signed a peace treaty with him. The war came to an end.

Tipu Sultan fighting the British

Tipu Sultan attacks Travancore...

Tipu spent the next few years strengthening his kingdom. He was a good ruler and was popular with his people. In 1789, Tipu attacked Travancore (a state in the south of India). The king of Travancore had the support of the British. The British along with the Marathas and the Nizam of Hyderabad came together to destroy the power of Tipu. The war went on for 2 years and then Tipu realized that he could no longer fight alone. He signed a peace treaty with his enemies and the war came to an end in 1792. Tipu had to give away half of his kingdom to his enemies. Tipu's half of the kingdom was divided between the British, the Marathas and the Nizam.

The death of Tipu Sultan...

Even after this defeat, Tipu was not discouraged. He spent the next 6 years improving his military and financial power. During this time, the British sent Lord Wellesley as the governor general. Wellesley wanted to crush Tipu's power before it could become a danger to the British. With the help of the Marathas and the Nizam of Hyderabad, the British attacked Tipu Sultan. The brave 'Tiger of Mysore' was left alone to face his three powerful enemies. In 1799, Tipu died defending his capital, Seringapatnam.

Tipu Sultan was not only a brave warrior but also a great king. He worked hard for the welfare of his kingdom and made his kingdom a truly modern state. Unlike other Indian rulers of his time, he refused to trade his freedom by entering into any agreement with the British. His dream was to build a strong and independent Mysore and he died in the pursuit of this dream.

THE SIKHS

(A new religion is found in the 15th century)

Guru Nanak, the founder of Sikhism (A.D. 1469 – A.D. 1539)...

In 1469, a baby boy was born to Tripta and Mehta Kalu Ram. An astrologer who saw the newly born's horoscope was so impressed that he actually touched the child's feet and predicted a great future for the child. The predictions turned out to be true. The child grew up to be **Guru Nanak** — the founder of a new religion, Sikhism.

Even as a child, Nanak was very different from other children. At school, he learnt things so fast that his teacher thought that he was a genius and would grow up to be a great man. He grew up and got married but still spent most of his time thinking about God and saying prayers.

Nanak worked as a store keeper and did his job well. His employer was delighted with him but Nanak himself was not happy. Then, one night, Nanak had a dream and saw God standing before him. 'Forgive me, O Lord! said Nanak 'I've done a great wrong'.

'What wrong have you done?' asked the Lord. 'I've thought only of this world,' he said, 'I've worked for money'.

'My blessing are with you,' said the Lord. 'Go out into the world and help all men'.

Guru Nanak

The very next day, Nanak gave up his job and gave away all his money and possessions. He wandered from place to place, spreading his teachings and ideas. Nanak taught the people to be honest, peace loving and contented. Many people liked his teachings and became his followers. His followers came to be known as the Sikhs.

There is an interesting story that reveals the lesson behind Guru Nanak's teachings. There was a rich man, Malik Bhago and Lalo, a poor farmer. Both of them invited Guru Nanak to stay in their house. Guru Nanak chose to stay in the poor farmer's house and the rich man demanded an explanation for this.

Guru Nanak asked both the rich man and the poor farmer to get some *roti* (food) from their house. Then taking Lalo's *rotis* in his right hand and the rich man's *rotis* in his left, he squeezed the two.

Everybody present was shocked to see drops of blood coming out of Malik Bhago's *rotis* and drops of milk coming out of Lalo's *rotis*. Guru Nanak then told Malik Bhago that his food was made from the earnings got by torturing and exploiting the poor and the weak, while Lalo's food was made from hard earned money. He advised Malik Bhago to earn by hard work and to serve the needy with a true heart.

The guilty man fell at the Guru's feet and begged forgiveness. The teachings of Guru Nanak are written down in a book called the **Adi Granth** which is the holy book of the Sikhs. Guru Nanak lived in the village of Kartarpur in Punjab. He died in 1539 but before he died, Guru Nanak chose one of his faithful disciples to carry on his work. He made him the next Sikh Guru. There were ten Sikh Gurus and Guru Nanak was the first Sikh Guru. Each Guru worked hard to develop and spread the religion of Sikhism.

Guru Nanak with Malik Bhago and Lalo

The Sikhs become warriors...

At first, the Sikhs were quiet and peaceful people, interested only in the worship of God. The Mughal emperor Akbar respected all religions and gave them a piece of land. Here, the Sikhs built a temple which is known today as the **Golden Temple**. Around this place grew a big city, which we today know as Amritsar. It is the holiest place of pilgrimage for the Sikhs.

But during the reign of Aurangzeb, things became different. Aurangzeb cared for no religion except his own religion Islam. Tegh Bahadur (the Ninth Guru) was the Sikh Guru then. Aurangzeb ordered Tegh Bahadur to give up his religion. When the Guru refused, he was killed.

Guru Gobind, the son of Guru Tegh Bahadur was the tenth and the last of the Sikh Gurus. He organized the Sikhs into powerful soldiers. The Sikhs started keeping *kirpans* or swords.

They promised to be ready at all times to defend their religion and their people. The Sikhs were given new names with the title 'Singh' added to them. 'Singh' means 'the Lion'.

When Guru Gobind Singh died, he told his people that after him there would be no Guru and they must accept the Adi Granth as their teacher. That is why the book is called 'Guru Granth Sahib'.

The Sikhs fought a long and bitter battle against the Mughals. It lasted for over a hundred years and thousands of Sikhs died. But the Sikhs refused to give up their religion.

Did You Know?
The holy book of the Sikhs, 'Adi Ganth' is considered the eleventh or the last Sikh Guru & thus it is called 'Guru Granth Sahib'.

Guru Gobind Singh

Ranjit Singh…

Later, the Sikhs were united again under the leadership of Ranjit Singh. He was short, frail and had only one eye, yet he was a born fighter and an excellent horseman. At the age of 18, he became the ruler of Lahore. Soon, he conquered Amritsar, Multan, Peshawar and added to his kingdom. He rebuilt the temple at Amritsar in marble and covered its domes with gold. Thus, the temple originally known as 'Harmandir Saheb' came to be called the 'Golden Temple'.

Ranjit Singh

Did You Know?

Ranjit Singh had the Harmandir Saheb covered with pure gold and thus it came to be called as the 'Golden Temple'.

Golden Temple

The British crushing the Sikhs

During this time, the British were the masters of the whole of India except Punjab. Ranjit Singh was a wise ruler and realized that there was no point in fighting the powerful British. So he remained friendly with them and it was agreed that the river Sutlej would be the boundary between their territories. Ranjit Singh ruled for 40 years and worked hard to make the Sikhs into a powerful group.

The British occupy the Sikh Kingdom...

After Ranjit Singh's death, there was confusion and chaos in the kingdom. The British saw this as an opportunity and attacked the Sikh kingdom. There were four bitter battles and finally the Sikh kingdom passed into the hands of the British. The famous Kohinoor diamond, which the Sikhs had won from the heirs of Nadir Shah, was taken away to England to adorn the British crown.

THE REVOLT AGAINST BRITISH RULE
(A.D. 1856 – A.D. 1858)

After the fall of Tipu Sultan, the British only had one powerful rival, the Marathas. But soon the Marathas were also defeated by the British. The British fought many wars and more and more areas came under their control.

The British Policies...

In 1786, Lord Cornwallis became the governor general. He introduced the policy of permanent settlement. This gave some people the permanent right to collect taxes from farmers. These people were called the Zamindars. The Zamindars in turn had to pay a certain fixed amount to the British every year. The Zamindars collected much more from the farmers than what they gave to the British. The Zamindars made huge profits and remained faithful to the British. But the poor farmers became poorer. They were not spared from paying heavy land taxes even in times of drought and famine.

Doctrine of Lapse...

In 1848, Lord Dalhousie became the governor general. He introduced the policy of Doctrine of Lapse. According to this policy, if an Indian ruler died without leaving a child, his state would pass into the hands of the British. During Dalhousie's term, seven Indian rulers died without male heirs and their states were added to the British empire. This treatment given to the Indian rulers was a great blow to the pride and dignity of the Indian people.

Tipu Sultan's sons being presented to Lord Cornwallis

Indians become angry with the British...

The Indian people became very angry with the greedy and unjust ways of the British. More and more wealth was going out of the country. Indian people even if better qualified and efficient were not given good jobs. The factories in England produced cheaper goods and flooded the Indian markets with them. Indian artisans and weavers were unhappy as nobody wanted their goods. The Indian princes and kings had lost their power. They were being treated badly by the British. This made them angry. Moreover, the Indian soldiers in the British army were also unhappy.

They had many complaints. They were paid less than the British soldiers. They could not rise to higher ranks in the army.

The first war of independence...

In 1857, a new rifle was introduced in the army. Its cartridge had a greased paper cover. The end of the cover had to be bitten off before the cartridge could be loaded into the rifle. The grease was made of mixed animal fat. This offended both the Hindu and Muslim soldiers. In Meerut, 90 soldiers refused to use the cartridge. They were dismissed and put into prison. Then the rest of the soldiers revolted. They killed their officers and marched towards Delhi.

The Sepoy Mutiny

Bahadur Shah Zafar

This revolt is known as the **Sepoy Mutiny** or the **First war of Indian Independence**. The revolt spread to Uttar Pradesh, Bihar and Madhya Pradesh.

The old and powerless Mughal emperor Bahadur Shah Zafar, was declared the emperor of India by the union of Laxmibai, Nana Saheb and Tantia Tope.

The British suppress the Revolt...

The British first attacked Delhi and after a fierce battle lasting six days, they captured the city and the palace. Bahadur Shah Zafar and his sons were taken as prisoners. The sons were later shot dead and the old emperor was sent away to Burma where he spent his last years in exile and misery. Then the British suppressed the revolts in Kanpur and Lucknow. But the struggle was not over.

The Brave Rani of Jhansi....

One of the brave and capable leaders of the revolt was Laxmibai, the Ran of Jhansi.

In 1854, Lord Dalhousie sent his officers to bring Jhansi under British rule. Gangadhar Rao, the king of Jhansi had died leaving behind a 6 year old adopted son. The British refused to accept the adopted son as the prince (as per their policy of Doctrine of lapse which we read on page 144). Jhansi was taken over by the British. The 17 year old Rani Laxmibai was given a pension and was allowed to live in the palace. During the next 3 years, the Rani was forced to live quietly in the palace on the pension received from the British.

In 1857, the soldiers at Jhansi rose in revolt. They captured the fort and killed the British officers.

Rani Laxmibai

Tantia Tope

In March 1858, the British attacked Jhansi. The Rani along with her soldiers tried to defend the fort. But the British managed to capture the fort. However, the Rani, dressed as a man, managed to escape. Tantia Tope who led the revolt in Kanpur also joined Rani Laxmibai. Together they attacked the British but were defeated. Then, Rani Laxmibai along with Tantia Tope attacked Sindhia, the ruler of Gwalior and captured his fort.

The British came to the help of Sindhia and attacked Rani Laxmibai. Rani Laxmibai fought bravely but could not hold out against the might of the British. Rani Laxmibai fought for ten hours at a stretch and at last a British soldier shot her in the chest. The brave queen died fighting for the independence of her Jhansi.

Tantia Tope escaped and carried on the struggle for a while. But, finally his companion betrayed him and Tantia Tope was hanged. On 8th July 1858, fourteen months after the outbreak at Meerut, the British had suppressed the revolt.

There were many reasons for the failure of the revolt. The most important reason for its failure was that the revolt broke out before its actual fixed date, 31st May 1857. It broke out on 10th May and thus it was not properly planned. This helped the British crush the revolt. Also many Indian rulers like Sindhia of Gwalior and Jung Bahadur of Nepal remained loyal to the British and helped in crushing the revolt. Moreover, the south of the country and even in the north, Punjab and Bengal, did not rise in revolt.

But this revolt became a symbolic event as it was the biggest and the only widespread rebellion against British rule. It had the support of Indian people from various castes, classes and religion. Hindus, Muslims, peasants, soldiers, all came together to drive away the British from their country.

Rani Laxmibai fighting the British

AWAKENING OF INDIA

(A.D. 1858 – A.D. 1900)

Although the revolt of 1857 failed, it woke up the Indians to face the situation. 'Why should a few foreigners rule over millions of Indians?' the Indian asked themselves. 'Why should a tiny country like England control a vast subcontinent like India?'.

The British had introduced western education in India. The ideas of freedom and equality that the British taught in their schools were in great contrast to what was actually going on in India. The British thought of themselves as superior to the Indians. They had special carriages in trains, did not allow Indians to mix with them as equals and refused Indians to be the judges in the courts.

By the 1880's there were almost 478 newspapers being published in Indian languages. These did not just print news but began to criticize government policies of the British. There was now a desire among Indians to think and act independently. Indian people began to give up blind faith in ancient customs and traditions. Many social evils like *Sati*, (burning of widows) female infanticide (practice of killing girl babies), not allowing widows to remarry, were discouraged. The Indians developed a modern and broad outlook. Some of the leading reformers who influenced the people were Raja Ram Mohan Roy, Swami Vivekanand, Swami Dayanand Saraswati, Ishwar Chandra Vidyasagar, Annie Besant and Sir Syed Ahmad Khan.

Swami Vivekanand

Raja Ram Mohan Roy

Annie Besant

Sir Syed Ahmad Khan

The Indian National Congress...

The educated Indians came together and decided to form an organisation. Through this, they wanted to tell the British what Indians as a nation felt. Thus, in 1885 an organization called the Indian National Congress was born. In the beginning, the Congress was supported by a group of Englishmen. The most important among them was Allan Octavian Hume, who is called as the father of the Indian National Congress. The Congress soon spread all over the country. People from different religions and regions, men and women, rich and poor, villagers and city people became its members. It soon became the voice of the nation. The most important leader of the congress in its earliest days was **Dadabhai Naoroji**. Through his books and speeches he described how poor our country had become because of the British. He declared that India's goal was *Swarajya* or Freedom.

Bal Gangadhar Tilak

Freedom is my birthright and I shall have it

The other important leaders were Surendranath Banerjee and Gopal Krishna Gokhale. These people believed that by peacefully appealing to the British government, the British could be forced to accept Indian demands.

During this time, there were also some other popular leaders like **Bal Gangadhar Tilak**, **Bipin Chandrapal** and **Lala Lajpat Rai**. They together were known as Bal-Pal-Lal. They had no faith in the good intentions of the British government. They taught the Indian people to believe in their own strength and be prepared for any sacrifice for their country. Bal Gangadhar Tilak tried to make the common man participate in the freedom struggle. "Freedom is my birthright," he declared, "and I shall have it." He used his newspaper *Kesari* to spread his ideas.

Dadabhai Naoroji

Indians burning foreign goods

The British trick of Divide and Rule...

The Indian National Congress became a strong and truly national organization. The Indian people were becoming united to attain freedom.

Seeing the situation, the British played a trick to divide the people and weaken the freedom movement. Lord Curzon decided to divide Bengal into two parts. The division was in such a way that one part would have mostly Hindus and the other part mostly Muslims. It was clear to all that the partition of Bengal was to the advantage of the Muslims. The British wanted to set the Hindus against the Muslims.

The Swadeshi and Boycott movements...

The Congress decided to take action against this decision. The congress now had two parts – the Moderates led by Dadabhai Naoroji, Gopal Krishna Gokhale and Feroz Shah Mehta and the Extremists led by Tilak, Lajpat Rai and Bipin Chandrapal. The two groups united to oppose the partition of Bengal. There were more than 2000 public meetings to protest against the division of Bengal. The Swadeshi and Boycott movements were started. The Indian people boycotted (stopped using) foreign goods and used only the goods made in India (*swadeshi* goods). At many places, people burnt foreign goods.

Rabindranath tagore

Rabindranath Tagore appealed to the people saying, "The government is determined to divide us. But our hearts will never be severed. Let us tie *rakhis* on 16th October (the day of the partition) for *rakhi* is the symbol of unity."

'Swadeshi' and 'Boycott' movements changed the tone of the national movement. Up till now there were polite requests for reforms by well mannered, educated Indians. Now they were replaced by demands backed by the pressure of thousands of common people.

These movements had such an impact that soon the washermen refused to wash foreign clothes. October 16, 1905 the day of partition was a day of mourning throughout Bengal. The Indian people boycotted not only foreign goods but also government schools, courts of law and renounced titles and government posts. The boycott movement continued till 1908 after which the British managed to finish it through more and more aggressive measures. There was *lathi* charge on people and many Indian leaders were also arrested. However, three years later, the British reunited East and West Bengal.

But the purpose of the British trick had been achieved. The agitation against the partition was mostly carried out by Hindus. This made the Muslims worry about themselves. The Muslims felt they should set up their own political organization as against the Congress. So in 1906, the **Muslim league** was established by Nawab Salimullah.

The Congress and the Muslim League

FREEDOM FIGHTERS
(In the 20th Century)

The boycott and swadeshi movements failed in driving away the British. This made the young people of India feel that may be violent methods could make them get freedom. These young freedom fighters set up secret training centres in Bengal. They killed British officers and destroyed British government property.

One of the great freedom fighter of this time was **Chandrashekhar Azad**. Azad joined hands with another brave man named **Bhagat Singh** and motivated the Indians to fight for their freedom. Many young Indians joined the freedom struggle. But the majority of Indians were peace loving people and did not take to violence to get Independence.

Did You Know?
Chandrashekhar was barely thirteen or fourteen years old when while taking part in a procession, he was arrested. When the magistrate asked his name, Chandrashekhar answered, "My name is Azad, which means free." Thus, he came to be called as Chandrashekhar Azad.

Did You Know?
Bhagat Singh killed Saunders, the British police officer who had earlier beaten up the popular Indian leader Lala Lajpat Rai.

Chandrashekhar Azad

Bhagat Singh

MAHATMA GANDHI

(The Father of the Nation-A.D. 1869 - A.D. 1948)

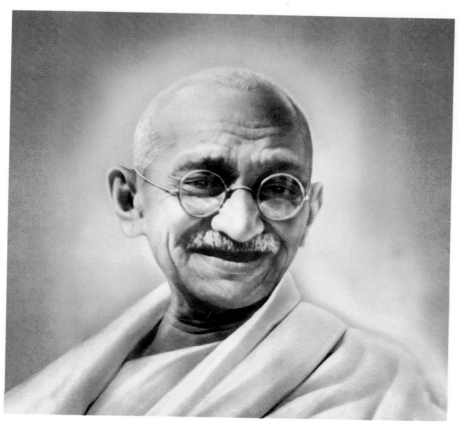

Mahatma Gandhi, the Father of the Nation

Mohandas Karamchand Gandhi was born in 1869 in Porbandar. He was a very shy and ordinary child. Like most children, he went to school and just about managed to pass his exams. At the age of 13, he was married to Kasturba.

Gandhi learns the value of truth...

From an early age, Mohandas always tried to speak the truth. But in his early teens he fell into bad company. He started to smoke, eat meat and steal money. However, he soon realized that his parents will be very hurt when they would come to know of this. So he decided to tell his father. He wrote out a letter to his father confessing his ill deeds and promising never to repeat them. His father read the letter and became very sad. But he did not scold his son. Mohandas felt very sorry that he made his father sad. But he was also grateful to his father for not scolding him. This incident taught Gandhi the value of truth.

LESSONS TO LEARN...

HONESTY IS THE BEST POLICY

Gandhi being ill treated in South Africa

Gandhi, the lawyer...

When Gandhi was 19 years old, he went to England to study law. After studying law, he came back to India. He tried to practice law both in Bombay, and Rajkot, but was a complete failure! In his first court case he was so nervous that he was unable to speak at all.

Did You Know?

Once, in South Africa, Gandhi was thrown out of a train as he was travelling in the first class compartment which the white South Africans believed was only reserved for them. Gandhi protested as he had a first class rail ticket. At this he was beaten and humiliated by a white police man. This incident sparked off the idea of 'Satyagraha' in Gandhi's mind.

Gandhi in South Africa...

In 1893, when Gandhi was 24 years old, he went to South Africa for a legal case. In South Africa, the white people treated the Africans and Asians very badly. They were not allowed to walk on the same pavements as the white people or travel in the same coaches in trains. If they did, they were insulted, tried and even jailed. Gandhi himself was ill-treated by the white people.

Gandhiji starts Satyagraha...

Gandhi decided to stay in South Africa and fight for justice. He stayed for 22 years in South Africa and devoted himself to improving the conditions of Indians living there. He showed the people a new way of fighting injustice. Gandhi believed in getting justice through peaceful methods. If he thought a law was unfair, he believed it was not wrong to break it and accept cheerfully any punishment given. He said that if one had to hurt someone to get something, then that thing was not worth having at all. Gandhi called his way of fighting without violence as 'Satyagraha' which means *the force of truth*. Gandhi was a firm believer in truth and nonviolence.

The start of Satyagraha

163

Gandhiji returns to India...

In 1915, Gandhi returned to India. He saw that the Indians were being ill-treated under the British rule. Gandhi stressed that Indians should be united against the British.

The First World War...

During this time, the First World War broke out. Britain, France, Russia and some other countries were on one side and Germany was on the other. Britain wanted help from India and promised that Indians would get more rights when the war was over. Over a million Indians volunteered to fight in the war on behalf of Britain. The Indians faced many problems during the war like food shortages and rising prices. But they hoped that after the war their conditions would improve. In 1919, the war was over and the British introduced some reforms. These reforms were so insignificant that Indians were very disappointed. Gandhiji first requested the government not to introduce these reforms. On being ignored, he called on the people of India to break the new laws. The Indians carried out demonstrations, strikes and public meetings. The British killed hundreds of people and thousands were arrested.

Jallianwala Bagh Massacre

Did You Know?

India Gate was built to honour the memory of Indian soldiers who had died fighting for the British during the First World War and the Third Afghan War.

Jallianwala Bagh...

The most brutal act of the British was perhaps the Jallianwala Bagh massacre. On 13th April 1919, at a place called Jallianwala Bagh in Punjab, 20,000 men and women gathered to hear their leaders. The British had declared all public meetings illegal. The British officer General Dyer decided to teach Indians a lesson. He came to the meeting with 150 full armed soldiers and blocked the only exit of the ground. Without warning the people, he ordered his soldiers to open fire on the unarmed crowd. Since Jallianwala Bagh was surrounded by high walls on all sides, there was no way people could escape. There was nonstop firing and the firing stopped only when there was no ammunition left. More than 1,000 people were killed and over 1,200 were wounded.

The British praised General Dyer for his bravery. Gandhiji and the whole nation was shocked at this Brutal Act.

General Dyer

"Cooperation in any form with this British government is sinful," Gandhiji said. He declared 'Satyagraha' against the British.

This was the start of the Noncooperation Movement. People did not cooperate with the government and deliberately broke laws. Thousands of students left their schools and colleges. Many lawyers gave up practicing law. People burnt foreign cloth by making bonfire of it on the streets. Indians started wearing thick, rough *Khadi*, thus doing away with the difference between the rich and the poor.

Did You Know?
An excited Indian crowd set fire to a police station and burnt 22 policemen alive! This happened in Chauri Chaura in the district of Gorakhpur and greatly disturbed Gandhiji.

Nehru with Gandhi

During this time, another important person joined the freedom struggle. He was **Jawahar Lal Nehru**.

Jawahar Lal Nehru...

Jawahar Lal Nehru was the son of a rich lawyer. He was brought up in the manner of rich British boys. He studied in England and later came back to India. Gandhiji's ideas and talks greatly influenced him. He decided to join the freedom struggle. He gave up his wealthy lifestyle and took to wearing *Khadi*. He was one of Gandhiji's most dedicated followers.

Hindus and Muslims...

While the freedom struggle was spreading throughout the country, the relations between Hindus and Muslims were gradually growing worse. The British turned the Muslims against the Hindus by suggesting that *Swarajya* (freedom) for India would mean *Hindu Raj*. Under this, the Muslims would be dominated by the Hindus who were in majority.

The Civil Disobedience Movement...

In 1929, the session of the Indian National Congress was held in Lahore at the bank of river Ravi. At this session, the congress decided that it would not rest until India gets complete Independence or *Poorna Swaraj*. The Congress entrusted Gandhiji with leading a civil disobedience campaign against the British. Gandhiji decided to start his campaign by breaking the unjust **salt law**. Salt was freely available along the Indian coastline but the British had made the collection of salt an offence so that they could sell the salt that came from England. Gandhiji decided to break the salt law by making or collecting salt.

Statue of Dandi March in New Delhi

On 12th March 1930, with his followers from his *ashram* at Sabarmati, Gandhiji walked for over twenty five days covering nearly 300 kms and reached Dandi. Here, Gandhiji collected some water from the sea. He heated it and made five grams of salt. The salt was then auctioned and a businessmen from Ahmedabad bought it for Rs. 525. The salt law was broken.

Gandhiji breaks the salt law

Now, thousands of men and women started making salt and selling it in the streets, openly breaking the British law. The breaking of the salt law was only one aspect of the widespread civil disobedience movement. Soon it spread to other fields. Government officials resigned from their post, foreign cloth and liquor shops were picketed and every unjust law was broken. For the first time, women came out of their houses and joined the movement. The British tried to crush the movement. Many Indians were killed and many more were sent to jails. But the Indians became even more determined to get Independence.

Dr. BR Ambedkar

Did You Know?

The British tried to divide the Hindus into two groups - the higher caste Hindus and the untouchables. Gandhiji realized this trick of the British and with the help of B. R. Ambedkar, the leader of the scheduled castes, called for the removal of untouchability. Gandhiji gave a new name to the untouchables and called them 'Harijans', meaning 'the people of God'.

Muhammad-Ali-Jinnah

The Quit India Movement...

During this time, the second world war broke out. The British forced India into the war without consulting the Indian leaders. In August 1942, when Japan threatened to attack India, Gandhiji once again gave a call for a country-wide *Satyagraha*. He asked the British to quit India. He said, "If Japan attacks India, it is because the British has made India their military base." Gandhiji called out to the people to 'Do or Die'. It meant either we win freedom or die in the attempt.

The Quit India Movement spread throughout the country and united the Indians against the British. In the meantime, the Muslim league under the leadership of Muhammad-Ali-Jinnah declared that Muslims were a separate people and must have their own country called **Pakistan**.

Subhas Chandra Bose...

Meanwhile, one more great freedom fighter, **Subhas Chandra Bose**, who had always believed that the only way to drive the British out was the use of force, felt that India must take full advantage of the war. In 1943, he took over the leadership of the Indian Independence Movement in South-East Asia. He expanded and reorganized the *Azad Hind Fauj* or Indian National Army (INA) which had already been formed with the help of Indian prisoners-of-war who had fallen into Japanese hands.

At a meeting in Singapore, Bose took an oath to free India and his countrymen and said, "*Tum Mujhe Khoon Do, Main Tumhe Azadi Doonga,*" (meaning you give me blood, I will give you freedom.) His famous call to the people of India almost became a national slogan. The people realized that they will get freedom only if they are prepared to sacrifice their lives for it.

Troops from the INA advanced with the Japanese army to the borders of India. They crossed the Burma-India border in 1944 and planted the Indian flag at Moirang in Manipur in April. But then disaster struck. Torrential rains came down, communications were cut, and cholera and malaria swept through the army. The Japanese began losing ground on India's eastern frontiers. They were also being pushed back across the Pacific Ocean by the armed forces of the United States of America. Many officers of the INA were captured and brought to India. Some of them were tried for treason. Then the sad rumour was heard that Subhas Chandra Bose had died in an air crash. The treason trials failed in the face of the entire nation's opposition. Bose or *Netaji*, as he was affectionately called, and his INA, live on in the hearts of millions of Indians.

Subhas Chandra Bose

Netaji's death in an air crash

India gets Independence...

The British government announced in 1946 that they were willing to end their rule in India. The Muslim league pressed its demand for a separate country for Muslims, Pakistan. The differences between Hindus and Muslims could no longer be resolved. There were Hindu-Muslim riots in many places in which more than five lac people were killed. The British policy of divide and rule had borne fruit. All efforts to keep India united were unsuccessful. Gandhiji, Nehru and the other Congress leaders reluctantly accepted the idea of partition.

Transfer of Power

India became independent on 15th August, 1947. A separate country of Pakistan was created which included West Punjab, East Bengal, Sind and North-West Frontier province. Jawahar Lal Nehru became the first prime minister of India.

While the entire nation was enjoying its new found independence, the man most responsible for this great achievement, Mahatma Gandhi was away in Calcutta comforting the victims of Hindu-Muslim riots. Gandhiji vowed to devote himself to bring friendship between the Hindus and Muslims in India. But on 30th January 1948, Gandhiji was shot dead while he was on his way to attend his evening prayers in Delhi. This brutal act was done by Nathuram Godse, a Hindu communal fanatic.

Gandhiji taught truth, nonviolence and communal harmony but he died a victim of communal bitterness. For some people he appeared to be standing up for the Muslims who had caused the partition. They did not understand that his only ideals were of love, truth and nonviolence.

Gandhiji lived and died for his country and will always live in the hearts of millions of Indians. Gandhiji, who was also affectionately called *'Bapu'* (which means father in Hindi), is rightly remembered as the 'Father of the Nation'.

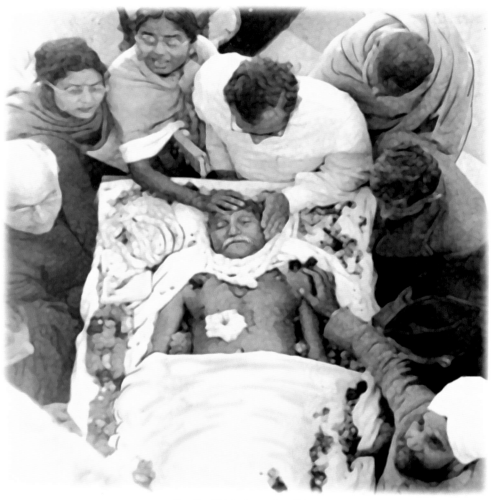

Death of Mahatama Gandhi

LESSONS TO LEARN...

Unity is strength

Gandhiji motivated the Indians to be united against the powerful British and attain independence. The British had a powerful army and modern weapons but were no match for the strength of the united Indians.

THE PROBLEMS OF INDEPENDENT INDIA

(Immediate problems of Independent India)

Sardar Vallabhabhai Patel

Immediate problems...

Independence did not mean all joy and celebration. There were many immediate problems which needed to be solved. Even after Independence there were about 600 big and small states ruled by *Rajas* and *Maharajas* who were earlier under the protection of the British. These rulers lived in great luxury. In Independent India, where everyone was equal, there was no place for Independent rulers. It was decided by the government to take over these states and merge them with the rest of the country. The rulers objected to this decision as this was a blow to their ego and power. But the task of merging these states was accomplished by **Sardar Vallabhabhai Patel** a devoted follower of Gandhiji.

Another immediate problem facing India was to provide food and shelter to the millions of people who had become homeless because of partition. The areas where they had their home had gone to Pakistan. The Indian government extended their help in settling them down in order to begin a new life.

INDIA, THE LARGEST DEMOCRACY

The Constitution of India...

Meanwhile, the Indian leaders prepared the new constitution of Independent India. The constitution lists the rights of every Indian and provides guidelines to help the government run the country. The new constitution came into force on **26th January, 1950** and India became a **Sovereign Democratic Republic**. Since then, 26th January is celebrated as the **Republic Day**. Dr. Rajendra Prasad became the first president of India.

Republic Day Celebrations

National Flag

Did You Know?

Jawahar Lal Nehru was the first Prime Minister of India and Dr. Rajendra Prasad was the first President of India.

Independent India also chose its national symbols. A replica of the Ashok Pillar at Sarnath in which 4 lions are sitting with their backs to one another, became the state emblem.

Our National flag is made of 3 colours - Saffron, White and Green. The white band in between has a chakra having 24 spokes in deep blue colour. Above it, there is the band of deep saffron and below it a band of deep green.

State Emblem

India, the largest Democracy...

India is now a Parliamentary Democracy. It means the people of India elect their leaders themselves who meet in what is called the **parliament** and make laws for the country. No more kings or foreign rulers. We rule ourselves through the leaders we elect.

Everyone above the age of 18 has a right to vote and is capable of electing the members of the parliament. These elected members form the government. No other country in the world has so many people involved in electing the leaders. That is why India is called the largest democracy.

Parliament House

India has been an independent country now for more than 60 years and has made tremendous progress in all fields. From being a country which could not make pins and needles, India has risen to become a great Industrial power. We now produce ships, aircrafts, automobiles, railways, computers, satellites and what not.

Of course, we are also facing the problems of population, illiteracy and poverty. But with our great vision, moral values and natural resources, our country will positively overcome all these problems.

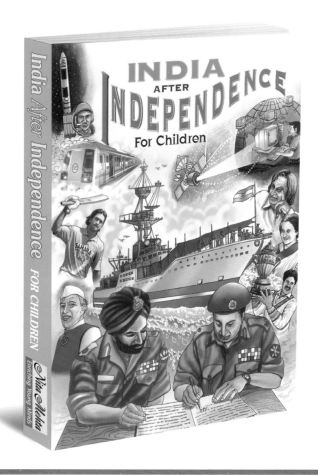